THE
INTIMATE
GOSPEL

OTHER BOOKS BY EARL F. PALMER

Salvation by Surprise
Love Has Its Reasons

THE INTIMATE GOSPEL

Studies in John

Earl F. Palmer

WORD BOOKS
PUBLISHER
WACO, TEXAS

For my mother and father

Contents

8   Contents

Preface

"Some dogma, we are told, was credible in the twelfth century, but is not credible in the twentieth. You might as well say that a certain philosophy can be believed on Mondays, but cannot be believed on Tuesdays. You might as well say of a view of the cosmos that it was suitable to half-past three, but not suitable to half-past four. What a man can believe depends upon his philosophy, not upon the clock or the century. If a man believes in unalterable natural law, he cannot believe in any miracle in any age. If a man believes in a will behind law, he can believe in any miracle in any age" (G. K. Chesterton, *Orthodoxy,* pp. 74–75).

John's Gospel is an intimate journal of a man who knew Jesus of Nazareth. It is a book about miracles and a book about the one who is the "will behind law," the one who is before and beyond everything else that is. This book of mine is about that intimate journal that St. John wrote in behalf of men and women of his century who wondered about the truthfulness and meaning of Jesus Christ.

Twenty centuries later, the questions being raised in our Tuesday of history are really very much the same as John's companions were asking on their Monday of history's week: Do I dare put my weight down upon the promises of Jesus? Are there miracles? Is the story about Jesus true? What after all is the meaning of life? Does God exist and is he able to speak for himself?

My own pilgrimage with these questions brought me at one point in my life into an unforgettable encounter with the Gospel of John. I remember then that I was surprised by the boldness of the book; I was embarrassed by its miracles; I was struck by its in-close and even interior portrayal of the life of Jesus. I feel the same way about John's Gospel today, and John's book makes as much sense today as it did yesterday. Its radical truthfulness is as fresh and

9

healing on the Tuesdays of our history as it was on the Mondays.

This commentary will seek to ask frankly two major questions of each paragraph of the Gospel. First of all, what does it mean within its own setting? Second, what does it mean for my life today? A study guide section is also provided to aid you in your own independent journey through John.

There are so many people who have been helpful to me. Let me express appreciation to the classes at Regent College, Vancouver; the Crucible Class, Berkeley; The Fuller Theological Seminary Extension Class. I owe a debt to my congregation at the First Presbyterian Church of Berkeley for their steady encouragement and challenge. My family—Shirley, Anne, Jonathan, and Elizabeth—are all great, not only because they keep me whole but in their role as theologians in residence. A very special "thank you" goes to Shirley my wife who typed the original manuscript, to Dorothy Gilroy who typed much of the rewrite sections, and to Mary Ruth Howes for her invaluable suggestions as my editor at Word.

EARL PALMER
Berkeley, California

Introduction

Let me share with you four underlying assumptions and goals that have guided my approach in the study of this remarkable book—The Gospel of John. First, this commentary seeks to understand the development of the Gospel of John as a reliable historical narrative of events in the life of Jesus Christ. Second, I will invite you to consider throughout the commentary some of the issues that have emerged in the history of New Testament studies as the major technical-critical questions concerning this Gospel. Our third goal will be to bring into focus the theological implications that are present in each part of the Gospel. That is to say, we will try to grapple with what the text means within the setting of the first century and across the two thousand years since then to our own century. The fourth goal is what I call the discipleship goal. I want continually to ask for myself, and I hope you will do so as well, the really vital and costly question: What does John's narrative about Jesus mean for my life here and now? I like the way Rudolf Schnackenburg put it: "Every commentary on John represents a scientific decision and a personal confession of faith" (*The Gospel According to St. John,* 1:3).*

This introduction will be as brief as it is bold. Throughout the commentary it will be my intent to establish and sustain, as well as I can, certain working premises that I feel you the reader deserve to know at the outset. At the same time and in the same way it will be my intent to develop en route what I hope will be helpful and convincing replies to critical opinions concerning the Gospel of John that are contrary to the conclusions that I now suggest.

---

*Complete information on books and authors cited in the text may be found in the bibliography.

11

This Gospel was written following the writing of the Gospels of
Matthew, Mark and Luke by a writer who was aware of the content of the Synoptic Gospels as well as their presence and circulation in the early church. The Gospel of John was probably written
near the time of the fall of Jerusalem at about A.D. 70. "All the concrete arguments for a late date for the Johannine literature have
now been dissipated" (W. F. Albright, *New Horizons in Biblical
Research*, p. 46).

The style of composition points to one writer of the book, and on
the basis of internal clues as well as several fascinating autographs,
we conclude that the original writer of this Gospel is the son of
Zebedee—the disciple John. In coming to this conclusion we are in
agreement with very early witnesses within the ancient church
such as Irenaeus, Clement, Tertullian.

The Gospel of John was written in very simple and clear Greek,
yet the flavor of the whole work and the idioms that underly the
book are Jewish. "The Semitic coloring will make one hesitate to
question his Jewish origin, while the correct Greek, which is impressive in its own way, forces one to suppose that he lived for a
long time in a Hellenistic environment" (see Schnackenburg's discussion). The witness we have from St. Irenaeus is that John lived
in Ephesus when the Gospel was written. Perhaps he went to
Ephesus sometime after the Apostolic Council of A. D. 49 (Acts 15).

John's Gospel is like Matthew, Mark and Luke in certain obvious ways. Each Gospel seeks to portray events in the life of Jesus,
beginning with the nativity as in Matthew and Luke, or with the
forerunner John the Baptist as with Mark and John. All of the
Gospel accounts tell of incidents and of teaching, of the choice of
disciples by Jesus, of the shadow of opposition to Jesus that
develops gradually and then cumulates through the events of Holy
Week to the cross. Each Gospel tells of the actual victory of Jesus
Christ over death and the grave.

But John's Gospel is also very different from Matthew, Mark
and Luke. John is a more theologically reflective book than the Synoptics; he reflects upon the importance of events more than the
others; he records fewer events but he will devote a long and intensive narrative (i.e., chapter 9) to a single incident. There are in
John extensive dialogues and speeches. For instance, only in John
do we hear in any detail of the arguments that are made against
Jesus by those who challenge his claims. Though there are figures
and illustrations recorded by John in the teaching of Jesus, there
are no parables of the kind found in the other Gospels. John is not

as concerned with the Galilean ministry of Jesus as the other writers and instead concentrates his attention on Jesus' Judean ministry.

John also takes great care with what appear to be small details, and this attention to detail becomes very helpful to the reader. Nathaniel Micklem makes this observation of the need that the Synoptic Gospels have for the perspective of John. "There is a superb objectivity about the writing of the synoptic evangelists. Jesus said this, he did that, there is no comment . . . but this very objectivity is a weakness from another point of view. . . . We are given little idea of what it was to see Jesus and to hear him, of the impression he made, of the atmosphere of strain which he inevitably created" (*Behold the Man*, p. 8). John's Gospel preserves for us those very interior, existential ingredients that are so important in order to really understand what is taking place and why.

Now we can appreciate why John Calvin said in his preface to his own commentary: "I am accustomed to say that this Gospel affords the key to open the door to the other gospels" (*Commentary on the Holy Gospel of Jesus Christ according to John*, p. 22).

I invite you to enter into the exciting and windy landscapes of the Gospel of John. When you read its sentences from an expectant stance, then the view is breathtaking. These months during which I have read, considered, and wondered about John, I have been confronted with many surprises. There is the awesome majesty of the Lord of Life whom John's great overture will name the very speech of God. And at the same moment this Lord turns out to be the Jesus at a pool called Bethesda who cares deeply about one lonely, isolated man, someone who looks to us more like a piece of human wreckage. I hope the various parts of this commentary that now follow will become an invitation to you to take a journey for yourself into John's own journey with Jesus Christ.

EARL PALMER

These opening sentences are like an overture to a great musical score in which vast themes are briefly stated.

1. In the Beginning
John 1:1–18

The Gospel of John begins with a song, like the overture to a great symphonic composition in which the eventual themes of the symphony are briefly stated and suggested, yet with stunning force. Since this opening hymn has a certain independence from the rest of the book, interpreters have long given special attention to these few sentences. Whereas the introduction to Luke's Gospel and the Book of Acts are spare and so obviously introductory that they are totally dependent upon the narratives that follow, John's Gospel begins with a prologue that could be used in and of itself, in the same way as Tchaikovsky's "Overture to Romeo and Juliet" is a brief musical portrait, complete in itself, of the larger dramatic themes expressed in Shakespeare's epic love story.

The words that John uses in this prologue are not at first glance complicated or difficult to understand either in English or in Greek, yet those who have pondered the prologue have sensed in the simplicity of the sentences a depth that has profoundly challenged analysis or explanation. It is something like the intense stillness of blue that the first explorers of the ancient Mt. Mazama in Oregon felt when they stepped for the first time to the surprise embankment that surrounds Crater Lake. They saw a color of water in that great lake unlike any other clear water surface on the earth. It is the incredible depth of the water that makes the difference.

For the same reason, the opening poem of the Gospel of John has held a lasting fascination for all readers of the Gospel. The water is clear but deep.

"The Greek style of the fourth Gospel is highly individual. . . . The style remains not only clear but very impressive, charged with a repetitive emphasis and solemn dignity . . . in spite of the small vocabulary the reader never receives the impression of

15

an ill-equipped writer at a loss for the right word" (C. K. Barrett, *The Gospel According to St. John*, p. 5).

John's choice of words has stirred great interest. His language is Greek but the Jewish source behind the Greek is evident. So much so that a few interpreters have attempted to argue for an Aramaic original text behind the Greek text—that is, they argue, John first wrote the Gospel in Aramaic and then it was later translated into Greek. Though very few can accept such a view today, it does point up what is now the consensus among the most recent New Testament interpreters, and that is that John's vocabulary is influenced most heavily by the Old Testament and only secondarily by Greek thought and philosophy.

The argument for Aramaic origin was advanced in 1922 in the work by C. F. Burney, *The Aramaic Origin of the Fourth Gospel.* However, Adolf Scheatter in *Der Evangelist Johannes* (1930) more persuasively established that it is Hebrew idiom more than Aramaic that lies behind the Greek. "The writer thought in Semitic idiom while he wrote in Greek." "Perhaps the most important service of the Dead Sea Scrolls will be the demonstration which may be brought from them that John, the synoptics and Paul . . . draw from a common reservoir of terminology and ideas . . ." (W. F. Albright, "Recent Discoveries in Palestine and the Gospel of John," in *The Background of the New Testament and its Eschatology*, p. 169).

Rudolf Bultmann's 1941 commentary on John proposed just the opposite conclusion. It was his contention that the prologue is not so much Semitic as it is Greek, in fact Gnostic. He writes: "It is concluded, therefore, that the Evangelist has made a cultic community hymn the basis for the prologue," and "it is enough to recognize that the mythological figure of the logos has its home in a particular understanding of the world, namely, the Gnostic" *(The Gospel of John, a Commentary*, pp. 17, 24).

In this interpretation by Bultmann, the prologue of the Gospel is necessarily incorporated by John from basically a Gnostic source with which he is presumably familiar. The hypothesis of Bultmann has failed, however, to sustain its conclusions in the face of several assaults. First, the language analysis previously mentioned points more to a Jewish than to a Greek origin for its vocabulary. Second, the continual pressure of research places the date of John's Gospel much earlier than Bultmann could have expected in 1941. Third, the search for the Gnostic sources he proposed has led to greater and greater demonstration of the fact that Gnosticism is a movement that follows the New Testament, not a movement fully formed prior to the writing of the New Testament. Research has shown that there are protognostic or pregnostic outlooks and attitudes. We have extensive evidence for the fact that the New Testament writers do battle against protognostic positions. (See Earl F. Palmer, *Salvation by Surprise*, pp. 70–76.) 1 John 4: 1–3 is a good example of this contest. John argues in this passage that it is of vital importance for Christians to recognize that Christ has "come in the flesh." The Gnostic outlook would prefer a more "spiritual" Christ. But that is quite a different matter than the thesis proposed by Bultmann.

Therefore, my conclusion is that the prologue is unique and independent in itself, though integral to the whole book. The relationship is much like the brief overture to the musical *Oliver* is to the larger musical work. The evidence most strongly points to the same author at work in the opening music as in the remainder of the book. Songs like "Consider Yourself," "Where is Love," etc. are present in the overture, but not completed.

John's parenthetic style with running comments made for the benefit of the reader is present in the opening song as in the whole book. His vocabulary is essentially molded from a Jewish perspective, yet the word choice also shows sensitivity toward the Greek world. By this, I believe, he shows his concern to communicate with Greek readers, yet without compromising his basic world view convictions that he has discovered from the world of Old Testament thought and supremely from his teacher, Jesus Christ.

Now let us consider the text itself: "In the beginning was the Word." This dramatic opening will certainly remind his Jewish readers of Genesis 1. The book of the Law begins, "In the beginning God created . . . God said . . . " John uses the Greek word *logos* ("word") in the same way. This *logos* exists with God, and is God, and as in Genesis, the Word exists prior to the creation of the world.

In the prologue we become aware that John is holding back in his use of the name *Jesus Christ*. (See also 1 John 1:1–4.) *Logos* then becomes the first in a series of descriptive words that John will draw together in this opening hymn. The question is: What does the word *logos* mean to the various readers of the book, and why does John use it? To the Jew the idea of the *Word of God* is understood primarily in terms of authoritative, creative action and will. This is the case in Genesis where, by the *Word of God*, the creation occurs, and also in the prophets where, by the Word of God, his mighty will is made known to humanity.

For the Greeks who read this prologue, the word *logos* also has its own special significance. "The stoics thought that a divine principle of logos or reason is within and behind the universe, and maintains it in being and order" (R. H. Lightfoot, *St. John's Gospel and Commentary*, p. 53). Notice the sensitive way in which John addresses that reader who is culturally Greek and who brings to the prologue his or her own understanding of *logos* as that sense of reason or meaning which orders the whole of reality. He has made use of the simple though profound word *logos* (word) which has a rich meaning in both his own Jewish world of experience and also in the contemplative tradition of the Greeks. Seen then in the perspective of both traditions, John is communicating the following:

"In the beginning was *the speech.*" "In the beginning was *meaning.*" John Calvin draws together both of these intentions in his statement: "As to the Evangelist calling the Son of God *the Speech*, the simple reason appears to me to be, first, because he is the eternal wisdom and will of God; and secondly, because he is the lively image of His purpose" (*Commentary on . . . John*, 1:26). By the identification of the logos with God in the beginning, John has clearly taught the eternal preexistence of Jesus Christ. He further settles the matter by the statement, "all things were made through him." Later in the Christian era Gnostic teachers will deny this affirmation, and will seek to separate the Redeemer from the Creator. They will teach that an inferior deity is responsible for the creation of matter which for them then resolves the problem of evil in the world. But the New Testament and the Old Testament will have nothing to do with such a doctrine. The world itself is created by the good decision of God.

John's hymn presents the logos as personal. This is the force of the pronoun translated "through him." The logos is not a status of reality, as in Buddhist religious thought about ultimacy, or a divine impersonal power, as in current religious power and actualization movements. The logos is PERSON. Now we are at the radical center of the affirmation of the Bible. At the center of everything is the God of character who is in the profoundest sense "I am." He is the one who speaks for himself. "In the sense of Christian faith, God is not to be found in the series of gods. He is not to be found in the pantheon of human piety and religious inventive skill. . . . I said that God is He who, according to Holy Scripture, exists, lives, and acts, and makes himself known" (Karl Barth, *Dogmatics in Outline*, pp. 36, 37).

"In him was life . . . light." The two words *life* and *light* are now added to the song. Like the word *logos*, they have a universality about them which reaches across philosophical and religious systems. In a profound sense they represent the generic longings that emerge in every world-view. John simply states that the longings in all human beings for existence and truth are to be found in their author—God himself. When God speaks for himself, John tells us, life and light are bound up within the speech.

"The light shines in the darkness and the darkness has not overcome it." Now the brooding negative countertheme is introduced. We meet the reality of evil, here described as *darkness* (see this same theme portrayed by John in his first epistle, 1 John 1). Once again the awareness of the severe contest between good and evil is a universal awareness. The prologue does not explain the origin of darkness; it is assumed. This means that the existence of evil is somehow allowed by God within the creation. Theologically and philosophically the existence of evil is related to the freedom which God grants to the created order. Freedom which later in this song will express itself in the response of faith—"all who received . . . "—is now portrayed in its opposite possibility, by a bitter hostility to the will of God. This is what John calls darkness. Note, therefore, that the darkness portrayal is a freedom portrayal —the freedom to deny, to oppose. But there is a limit to the authority and power of darkness. It has not overcome the speech of God. God's power is still greater; it is by God's own wise decision that darkness is permitted to persist in its "no" to God's "yes." Therefore, by this description of the reality of the hostile "no" to God, we are assured that freedom is real because God has written it into the very symphony of reality. We may have preferred it to be otherwise, but the contest between good and evil is the way reality really is.

At this point John interrupts the song with the first of three footnotes. He tells the reader about John the Baptist who had the prophetic task of pointing to the light. The fact that the Gospel of John so clearly emphasizes that John the Baptist is not himself the light is an important evidence of the fame of John the Baptist even at the time of the writing of the Gospel, and perhaps is an indication that his followers have continued as a movement following his execution by Herod. Rudolf Bultmann even theorized that this prologue in its original poetic form may have come from this John the Baptist community (Bultmann, *The Gospel of John*, p. 18). This is how he explains the evangelist's interruptions of the poem.

The next paragraph in the poem (vv. 9-13) repeats parts of the first two paragraphs and then describes the result of faith in the life of the one who believes in God's name. *Name* here refers to the self-disclosure of God. John's hymn teaches that whoever receives God's own speech is granted by God's decision the spiritual birth into God's family. It is interesting that John's Gospel does not make use of the nationalistic kingdom language that so characterizes Matthew, Mark, and Luke; instead we have the language of the family.

The song comes to a triumphant close: "The Word became flesh and dwelt among us, full of grace and truth." Martin Luther poses the challenge of John's prologue: "There are people who can't stand a bodily God, as God became flesh for us. They want to have a spiritual God and boast of their use of *logos*, though the use of *logos* without the fact is a figment of the imagination" *(Luther's Works,* 2:197).

The logos that John praises in this opening hymn of the Gospel is not the figment of imagination, not the creative experience of the early Christians, not the highest and best thought of philosopher or theologian, not the mystical vision; John's claim is that the Word has become historically concrete and real. It is in witness to this historic breakthrough of the eternal Word that the song now comes to its dramatic crescendo; "Full of grace and truth." We know from later Gnostic writers that the words *full,* and *fullness— pleroma—*will play a key role in the Gnostic descriptions of divine revelations. Their specialized use of this term does not disqualify the word as far as New Testament writers are concerned (see Paul's use in Col. 1:19). John asserts literary authority over the word *pleroma, full,* in this text. In no way is his message jeopardized by his choice of a word which is probably already in use among the protognostic groups that begin to emerge early in life of the primitive Christian church.

Grace, charis, is a word John now uses to describe the surprising gift-love of God. The words *pleroma* and *charis* are not typical Johannine words and each appears only in this hymn in the Gospel. *Grace* is a word used extensively by Paul and Luke. Perhaps John has chosen the word precisely because *grace* as a word is so decisively used by these other two leaders of the early church.

Glory is used by John in its Old Testament sense as the mixture of wonder and authority that is always a reference to the presence of God and the disclosure of God's character. It was what Isaiah heard from the seraphim in his encounter with Yahweh (Isa. 6:3).

> Holy, holy, holy is the Lord of hosts;
> the whole earth is full of his glory.

In the phrase "grace upon grace," the connective word *anti*, translated here as "upon," usually means "opposite" or "in the place of." John has used this word *anti* in a remarkable way. He means that wherever you look—on one side or the opposite side, in one place or over against that place somewhere else—we will make the discovery that God's grace, his surprise love, is there ahead of us. Wherever we look or go, God's love is there by surprise.

John's final main point is that as John the Baptist bears witness to the logos and is, therefore, secondary to it, so Moses, who received the Law on Mt. Sinai, is also secondary to God's mighty speech. John's Gospel will show a continuing interest in Moses, and we shall meet him again as John's narratives unfold. The point is that Moses, and the Law given by God through him, is like the arc of a great circle which now in its completeness incorporates Moses' witness and life within its present vast sweep revealed in Jesus Christ.

Now finally, in verse 17, the name about which this Gospel will have the most to say is brought into the text, the name *Jesus Christ*. Jesus Christ is the very speech of God.

The Gospel of John has sketched in with a very few words several large themes. The whole created order owes its origin and its meaning to the decision of God, the very decision which has been with God from the beginning and before creation itself. This is the good news which invites each of us to welcome all that is within the created order as having meaning not dependent upon chance or randomness but because of the will of the Creator. The reality of evil is confronted, but its authority, though it may endanger and terrorize humanity, is not ultimate. The decision of God by which he makes himself known in life and light is greater than the power of darkness. Jesus Christ is the eternal speech of God, he can be known as truth, and his life can be experienced within our lives. These are the last themes that John dares to introduce within the poetry of his prologue.

Now we are ready for his book to unfold its narrative. We have so many questions to ask. If the prologue has made sweeping and radical affirmations, it has also challenged long-standing religious premises and practices. If we have read the prologue closely, some of us may be as troubled as others are convinced.

2. The People's Prophet
John 1:19-34

What an impressive individualist is John the Baptist! He is a few months older than Jesus of Nazareth and already has become a folk hero by the time of the start of Jesus' ministry. He has his own followers and he has created such a stir among the people that some wonder if he himself is not the Christ. The role that John the Baptist chooses to play is that of the one who prepares the way for the Lord. John does this in four ways.

(1) First, he announces the stern message of the judgment of God upon the sinfulness of mankind. Luke records a vivid portrayal of this crucial element in John's message, "You brood of vipers! Who warned you to flee the wrath to come?" (Luke 3:7). John's words are harsh, but the severity of the message does not diminish his popularity with the people. In fact, his prophetic promise is that when the Christ will come, the judgment he will bring will be even more intensive and complete than the stern language of his forerunner: "I baptize you with water . . . he will baptize you with the Holy Spirit and with fire. His winnowing fork is in his hand, to clear his threshing floor" (Luke 3:16–17). It is clear that John expects Jesus to complete in an overwhelming and total way what John is only speaking about with words and warnings.

When John the Baptist points to Jesus and exclaims, "Behold, the Lamb of God, who takes away the sin of the world!" (John 1: 29), it is important for us to remember that he speaks as much of the mighty warrior calf of Malachi 4 who will vanquish evil as of the lamb of Isaiah 53 who was to bear upon himself human sin. We must not miss this unmistakably apocalyptic ingredient in the message of John the Baptist. John is like Elijah in contest with the four hundred false prophets of Baal. We feel this continuous sense of battle in John the Baptist and in his predictions of the role that the one who is both before and after him will take.

(2) There is a second way in which John the Baptist prepares for Christ. It is represented in the baptism he offered to the people who came to hear him. His baptism is a sign of repentance and preparation for the coming of the Lord. It has ethical implications which become clear in his pastoral counsel to the soldiers in Luke 3, yet it is at the same time prophetic. You will note that in the Gospel of John, the writer does not really explain the baptism procedures of John the Baptist. He does not explain the repentance theme but rather chooses to emphasize the prophetic element: "I came baptizing with water, that he might be revealed to Israel" (John 1:31). That is, John's baptism as a ritual pointed to the Lord, as did his words. John's baptism is the event before the event, just as his role is to be like the friend of the bridegroom who rejoices to see his friend's wedding take place.

This is how John the Baptist describes his own ministry in his dialogue with the Pharisees (John 3:25). In this sense John's baptism is good news, and his stern words are good news in that they bring us "weary and worn out to the Redeemer" (Pascal). This is his mission—to point broken and discouraged humanity to the Light. "We cannot hear the last word until we have heard the next to the last word" (Dietrich Bonhoeffer, *Letters and Papers from Prison*, pp. 156–57).

(3) John the Baptist is significant in a third way. He plays a mysterious, intensely personal role toward Jesus himself. Each Gospel tells us of the baptism of Jesus by John—that wondrous incongruity, where Jesus, who had no need to submit for a baptism of repentance, yet insists that John baptize him at Jordan. It is in this submission of Jesus, his total identification with the crowds of ordinary people who had also come to the river, that a sign is given by God both to Jesus and to John: "This is my beloved son. . . . " John is privileged to share in that mystery. "I have seen and have borne witness" (John 1:34).

(4) John the Baptist as a theologian, as we will later note in chapter 3, gives another picture and a fourth way in which he is significant to the Gospel accounts. This can be described in terms of the personal character and context of his life and ministry seen in its own right.

John is a remarkable person and probably more famous in Judah than is Jesus himself. He has loyal followers, who journey in his behalf from his imprisonment by Herod to Galilee in order to quiz Jesus (Luke 7). They express to Jesus John's disappointment in the way Jesus is carrying out his ministry.

This is the towering figure who had been so sure of Jesus, who was the first to believe. He had announced Jesus as Christ, and he possessed the greatest faith: "He must increase, but I must decrease" (John 3:30), he had said. This same John, at the low moments of his imprisonment, is unsure of both Jesus and himself. "Are you he who is to come, or shall we look for another?" (Luke 7:19). He becomes the one who first doubts Jesus at a very profound level. The first who really believed; the first who really doubted. This enigma is John the Baptist. Within the agonizing mixture of these crises of conviction, John plays such a substantial role in sharpening our focus as to who Jesus Christ really is. Jesus is the one to whom John pointed as Lord, "the thong of whose sandal I am not worthy to untie" (John 1:27). And Jesus is the one to whom John turns with his hardest questions when he feels confused and disappointed by the way Jesus has chosen to walk and live and act as the world's Messiah.

Recent New Testament scholarship has focused considerable attention upon John the Baptist. Several questions have arisen: Is it John the Baptist's teaching which becomes the source that St. Luke makes use of in the canticles (songs) he records at the opening of his Gospel (i.e., the Magnificat, the Benedictus)? Do some of the Baptist's followers remain on after the death of John the Baptist and do they establish their own movement separate from the Christian church? We have evidence of this in Acts 19:24–25. This would help to explain the underscoring by the Gospel of John that John the Baptist is not the *light* that is coming into the world but the *witness* to the light (John 1:8).

The career of John the Baptist in this Gospel is not treated with as much information as in Luke. John does not repeat the Baptist's long speech (Luke 3:1–21). The Gospel does show an interest in where he conducted his ministry: he baptized "in Bethany beyond Jordan" (John 1:28), which may be a first-century local reference to what is now at or near Betharba. Later the Gospel tells us he "was baptizing at Aenon near Salim, because there was much water there" (John 3:23). This attention to detail is characteristic of the Gospel of John. One thing is sure—John the Baptist has captured the imagination of the people. He is a unique personality—not cautious and correct like the Pharisees, not hidden and isolated like the Essenes who live nearby at Qumran above the Dead Sea, not a Zealot terrorist, not hypocritical like the Sadducees. John is bold, clear, definite, ethically courageous, stern. Yet this powerful, lonely figure meekly humbles himself before Jesus— "I am not worthy to untie his shoe." In the Gospel of John he is the first witness to tell clearly who Jesus really is. His voice is the first voice of faith to herald the adult ministry of Jesus Christ. He will also be the first voice of the doubt of a friend which St. Luke preserves for us (Luke 7).

Jesus both fulfills and disappoints John the Baptist's expectations. Jesus is the Lamb of God, and John is sure of it. Yet as the Lord's ministry unfolds, Jesus does not do what the great prophet John had expected him to do. He is hardly the calf of Malachi trampling the wicked. For most of his public ministry Jesus stays at Galilee, except for short visits in Judea, and seems to evade the mighty prerogatives that are his to use. The vast winnowing fork, the fire, the power of the very Holy Wind of God are his, yet he has set for himself priorities that John the Baptist never expected.

The mixture of *fulfillment* and *disappointment* of the expectations of the people will become a very crucial element in the unfolding portrayal of the life of Jesus Christ in the Gospels. The fact that Jesus so marvelously disappoints all our expectations of what we think the Messiah should be is itself one of the most eloquent proofs of his true messiahship. Jesus is not possessed by our expectations, as he is not possessed even by the hopes and dreams of so great a man as John the Baptist. But in a way more profound and complete than John could imagine, Jesus did fulfill the portraits of both the calf of Malachi and the lamb of Isaiah. That fulfillment will now be our task to trace throughout the Gospel of John.

3. The Disciples
John 1:35-51

Now we meet the disciples. Throughout the Gospel they are called disciples and never apostles. This is one of those features that argues for an early date of composition. If we date the Gospel of John at 95 A.D., we would expect the more impressive term *apostle* rather than the ordinary common term *disciple*.

First we meet Andrew and an unnamed disciple. This unnamed person is simply described as one of the followers of John the Baptist. We believe he is the disciple John. This is the most logical conclusion in the light of the inflexible rule followed throughout this Gospel, which does not name the Apostle John in any place but refers to him by indirect means. This feature, referred to as the Johannine autograph, gives support to the tradition of the early church which credits this Gospel to the Apostle John, the youngest of the disciples' band, brother of James, and a relative of Andrew and Peter.

John has added a clarifying piece of information to what we already know of the call of the disciples from Matthew, Mark and Luke. He points up that this early encounter with Jesus at the Jordan takes place prior to the call of the disciples at the Lake of Galilee, a call which in the other Gospels is portrayed as sudden and without preparation. He also makes it clear that Andrew and John were followers of John the Baptist prior to following Jesus. Now, from John's account, we know of this earlier meeting by John, Andrew, and Peter with Jesus. John insists on this chronological order by the phrase "the next day." The dialogue is plain and uncomplicated. In fact, after the symphonic poem of 1:1–18, and the dramatic pronouncement of John the Baptist in 1:19–35, this part is in such sharp contrast that we feel somewhat taken aback, even let down. Perhaps we expected a more absolute call to

the disciples. Watch closely as John's Gospel sets such expectations aside.

Jesus asks the two men what they seek, and they ask, "Where
are you staying?" Jesus then invites them to "come and see" and
they do. Later on at Galilee, Jesus will ask them to drop their nets,
leave everything and follow him—but now at the very beginning of
their journey he invites them simply to consider who he is.

It takes time to weigh the totality of the prophetic announce-
ment of John the Baptist, and Jesus respects that need. In fact
what impresses me most in this narrative is how plain and ordinary
is the dialogue. This means that the disciples of Jesus Christ begin
their Christian pilgrimage by single, very ordinary steps. Jesus begins where they are, and it is evidently with their questions and
their conclusions that he grapples. It is Andrew who calls Jesus
Messiah. It is Philip who describes with his own theology who
Jesus is to his friend Nathanael. Jesus' words are directed toward
them—he tells them who they are! Simon he names "Rocky."
Nathanael he calls the open-faced Israelite. The fact that Jesus
knows Nathanael so well is what deeply impresses Nathanael, and
the Lord marvels at how quickly he has switched from cynicism—
"Can anything good come out of Nazareth?"—to faith—"You are
the King of Israel!"

Only after Nathanael's confession does Jesus confirm his faith
with the mysterious messianic statement reminiscent of Jacob's
dream (Gen. 28:12). He introduces it with the Greek words *amēn,
amēn,* translated "truly, truly," by the RSV. Our English word
amen is a transliteration of the Greek, which itself carries over the
same word, sound for sound, from the Hebrew *amen.* The Hebrew
word means "foundation, rock, fortress." "Amen, amen, I say to
you, you will see greater things than these." And he uses for the
first time in this Gospel the messianic title from Daniel in reference to himself: "You will see ... angels of God ascending and
descending upon the Son of man."

Jesus wins these men to himself, and yet, as this dialogue shows
us, he does not take away from their own uniqueness or freedom. If
anything, their encounter with him has heightened their separate
qualities. Jesus affirms the directness of Nathanael, and the nick-
name given to Simon is an accurate appraisal of the person he is
and will become.

Who make up the band of followers that surround Jesus
throughout his ministry? In John's Gospel the twelve disciples are
not listed in any text as they are in Mark 3:13-19:

Simon whom he surnamed Peter; James son of Zebedee and John the brother of James, who he surnamed Boanerges, that is sons of thunder; Andrew, and Philip, and Bartholomew, and Matthew, and Thomas, and James the son of Alphaeus, and Thaddaeus, and Simon the Cananaean, and Judas Iscariot, who betrayed him.

Though this list as such is missing in John, there are included by John more in-depth glimpses into several of the twelve, in addition to others of the wider band of the men and women who followed Jesus. John's Nathanael is probably Bartholomew in Mark's list. John gives us several important insights into Philip, Nathanael, Andrew, and Thomas which help us really understand these disciples. Apart from John's Gospel, very little would have been known of these four.

What amazing contrasts within this first chapter of the Gospel of John! It begins with the symphonic-like prologue, introducing to us a great and complex musical score, and focusing primarily on the answer to one great question—who is this Logos of God? Then the interlude in which the strange enigmatic figure of John the Baptist stalks upon the stage, to turn every eye to the great center-theme of the whole symphony. Then the first surprise—one of many that will greet us at every new development of the narrative: Jesus is not like we expected him to be. The Jesus we meet through Andrew is conversational rather than triumphal; he is a friendly listener drawing out real men in a real encounter, spending the day with them, finding out who they are, nicknaming them. It is as if, following the majestic chords of the prologue and the great theme of John the Baptist, what we now hear is a melody line so simple and spare that at first it may elude us completely. But this is the Jesus Christ we meet.

At a Galilean wedding, Jesus begins his public ministry with an event that lets us see what God is like.

4. Invitation to a Wedding
John 2:1–11

Cana is a location mentioned only by John in the New Testament. It is probably the site Khirbet Qana some nine miles north of Nazareth. What happens there begins with a brief conversation between Jesus and his mother. She tells Jesus about a shortage of wine.

Recent studies into first-century wedding customs may help us to understand this question to Jesus by his mother. Wedding feasts would ordinarily last seven days, and the guests were expected to bring a present of wine. (R. E. Brown mentions the research of J. D. M. Derrett. See Brown, *The Gospel According to John*, pp. 97–110.) It is possible that Jesus and his disciples had failed to bring with them their present, and his mother intends only to remind Jesus of that omission.

Whatever is the reason for Mary's initial statement to Jesus, the Lord's reply is larger than her question, and goes far beyond what the reader might expect from the dialogue. He begins with a common Semitism, literally, "What to me to you." The "O woman" is not disrespectful but a title in ordinary usage. Then he expands his sentence far beyond the natural limits of the conversation by the heavy sentence, "My hour has not yet come."

How are we to interpret this dialogue? One result of this encounter is that the relationship between Jesus and his mother has been altered. There is an abrupt setting apart of Jesus from his natural relationships in a way similar to the Nazareth incident recorded in Luke's Gospel, except that the town-mates of Jesus in Luke's account (Luke 4:16–30) do not trust Jesus' decision, whereas his mother does. Within John's Gospel the mother of the Lord will not again take a significant role until the hour at the cross when Jesus Christ tenderly commends her to the disciple John and John to her (John 19).

29

Mary responds to the statement of Jesus as if she understands and is satisfied. She withdraws from the event, after instructing the servants to do what Jesus tells them.

John now gives to his readers the detailed information concerning the volume capacity of the stone jars. First-century practices and concerns for washings and rites of purification are now well-known. The Dea Sea Scrolls contain elaborate instructions concerning rites of purification. The traditions of washings go back to Leviticus 11:29–38 and are continued into the first century. Note Mark's comment (7:3–4): "For the Pharisees, and all the Jews, do not eat unless they wash their hands, observing the tradition of the elders; and when they come from the market place, they do not eat unless they purify themselves; and there are many other traditions which they observe, the washing of cups and pots and vessels of bronze."

At the instruction of Jesus, the servants draw out water, and take it to the headwaiter. It is they who discover that a miracle has occurred when the headwaiter complains to the bridegroom that the best wine has been held back.

With this statement of the headwaiter, the incident is over, except that John makes his own theological comment about the event. Such comments form an important characteristic of John's style throughout the Gospel. John tells his readers that this was the first of the *signs* of Jesus done at Cana, that it bears witness to the glory of Christ, and that the result of the sign was that the disciples believed in him. The signs in John are like the Old Testament sign of the exodus, meaningful in itself, yet pointing beyond itself to the larger foundation beneath it.

John tells us that something about this incident showed the glory of Jesus Christ. This word *glory* is first used in John's Gospel in the prologue: "we have beheld his glory, glory as of the only Son from the Father." We observe then that the word in its Old Testament sense has to do with the mystery of the presence of God himself. It is used in this same sense throughout the Gospel. That is, *glory* has to do with the revelation of the character of God. When we are enabled to see who God is and what he is like, we have witnessed his glory—his real presence. In other words, there is a breakthrough of the very character of God in this sign. That is John's point. The question is: What is the breakthrough that this event shows? Let me draw together five threads.

(1) The unique nature of the ministry of Jesus Christ is clearly asserted. Jesus speaks of *his* hour which is independent of every other relationship and every other hour. In the baptism of Jesus at

Jordan he is identified with all people. Now he is revealed as totally separate and alone upon a journey that only he may undertake. In this sense, there is also a permanent separation established between Jesus and his mother. She trusts in him as the Lord as she accepts this fact. At Nazareth, the people of Jesus' hometown did not have such faith.

(2) The incident shows the authority of Jesus to do signs as Elijah had done them many years before. Yet this sign at Cana is quiet and marked with a restraint and understatement that is itself to be a characteristic mark of the way Jesus carries out his ministry. According to John, the sign might have been missed had not the headwaiter made an issue of the better wine. Then it is that the servants explain the strange chain of events, and with their excited account the word is out.

(3) The sign itself is significant as a sign of transformation: the common water becomes the best wine. What Jesus touches he will transform. St. Paul expresses it this way: "If anyone is in Christ, he is a new creation" (2 Cor. 5:17).

(4) Jesus Christ has authority even over the natural order, over the processes of creation.

(5) The sign is celebrative and joyous in contrast to the gravity and starkness of John the Baptist. Jesus begins his ministry at Cana by showing his concern for the feelings of a young couple on their wedding day.

The sign is not exhaustive; it does not show everything of the purpose and nature of Christ. But it is a breakthrough of the inner character of Christ that the disciples are able to understand and to which they respond. That response John calls faith. Therefore, in this incident we have from John an opening definition of faith as the response of the disciples to the disclosure of Jesus Christ. Moreover, the disclosure came to them in terms that they could understand.

We must ask one further question of the narrative that is important for our consideration of this and the remaining miracle accounts in John's Gospel. The question is this: *Did the event happen?* Let me pose this question in another way. Is this sign at Cana a sign given by Jesus Christ himself who acts as John has narrated the scene, or is it the community of faith creating a story, at some later date, to tell in human terms the meaning of the eternal gospel? In the one case the event and its meaning are inseparably combined; in the second case the eternal truth stands by itself and the narrative of the "event" is, strictly speaking, secondary to the truth it illustrates. In the one case, *sign* is used in a Hebrew way as the Hebrews thought of signs; for instance, the exodus—an event given by God himself, actual and historical in its own right, and yet pointing beyond itself to the deeper reality of God's decision that lay beneath it. In the other case, *sign* is used in much the same way as Plato's shadows dancing upon the wall in his parable of the cave (*The Republic*, VII, 515). These have an apparent reality but only in the sense that they reflect or shadow a reality outside of the cave.

Before we are able fully to discuss the issues these questions pose, we must put into perspective some of the ways in which New Testament books have been interpreted. The method of interpretation of biblical texts called form criticism, which has had a very great influence on New Testament studies during this first half of this century, is convinced that the most important question to ask of any Gospel account concerns its relationship to the faith of the early church. The point of view that operates within form criticism is that the convictions of the early church, their beliefs about the eternal good news—their kerygma (preaching content) —is what stands as the motivational foundation determining what material went into the New Testament books. In other words, what the early believers wrote as scenes and incidents in the life of Jesus Christ was determined most of all by the faith of the writers themselves.

From such an interpretive stance, our principle concern in studying this Cana narrative would be to wonder what doctrine in the early church needed the support which such an account as the water-to-wine story would aid or illustrate. Would early sacramental teaching concerning the Lord's Supper benefit? Or perhaps the story might act as a Christian reply to the common Greek myths of water-to-wine miracles, such as the Greek traditions of the god of vintage, Dionysius. In his commentary, C. H. Dodd works through the former point, and from such a critical methodology he writes: "The story, then, is not to be taken at its face value. Its true meaning lies deeper . . . as a sign which sets forth the truth that with His coming, the old order in religion is superseded by a new order" (C. H. Dodd, *The Interpretation of the Fourth Gospel*, pp. 297, 299).

This method of interpretation works from the believing community that writes the document back to the document. I believe that such a method has useful features which make good sense in seeking to understand the early church realities, but it must be very cautiously applied. It has very serious dangers, where the interpreter is tempted to reconstruct the New Testament texts upon the basis of what he supposes their usefulness to be to the faith of the early church. It is the interpreter, then, who becomes the arbiter of what that core of faith really is, and with this advantage he is able to control fairly well the New Testament documents themselves. The result has often been a highly speculative approach to every text. T. W. Manson explains the dangers: "To speak candidly, I find myself, after a good deal of labor in this field, being gradually driven to the conclusion that much that passes for historical study of the life of Jesus consists not in asking of any story in the tradition: 'Is it credible in itself?' but, 'What motive could the church have had for telling this tale?' which can easily become the question: 'What motives led the church to invent it?' The danger is that what is entitled 'Life of Christ' or the like should turn out to be in fact a psychological novel about a large number of anonymous members of the primitive church" (T. W. Manson, *Studies in the Gospels and Epistles*, p. 7).

When it comes to the Gospel of John, the critic should move with great care. "The Gospel stubbornly refuses to be dismembered, refuses to be divided into history and interpretation. The history invades the interpretation and the interpretation pervades the history" (E. C. Hoskyns, *The Fourth Gospel*, "Introduction"). The accounts in John are not written as if the intent of the writer is to provide tales which illustrate truths. The writer's attention to small details—such as the amount of water that the stone jars could hold, and the precise geographical notations that play such an important part in the narration—is typical of historical narrative.

Moreover, the historical earnestness of John's accounting is obvious in every sentence. The document is written as if the events happened as told. Certainly John chooses what events to include, and he reflects upon the theological importance of the Cana incident; but in his account it is the incident that inspires the faith and not a believing writer who, as a devout novelist, creates inspirational incidents. I believe that C. K. Barrett is very wide of the mark in his statement where he comments upon John's purpose in writing the Gospel: "Accordingly, 'These are written that ye may believe' (20:31), not that ye may have a reliable account of what Jesus really did and thought, but that, whatever the details of his ministry may have been, ye may believe" (*The Gospel According to St. John*, p. 3). In this conclusion we see that Barrett is dangerously close to creating a break between the historical *event* and the *eternal faith*. This may, in fact, be his own theological conclusion, but he cannot fairly say it of the intent of the writer of the Gospel of John. John is serious and careful throughout the account about the details and data that are the raw material of true historical documents.

This issue has again become a very important question for interpreters of John in the light of the massive documentary and archeological evidences that have flooded in during the last fifty years and have continued to sustain the integrity of the Gospel texts and to move dates of authorship earlier and earlier into the first century. The evidence we do have is that the early church is dependent for its faith upon the event, Jesus Christ. We do not have evidence of the Gospel writers creating a "Life of Jesus" narrative to support doctrine. We do see that phenomenon in the Gnostic books of the second century but not in the Gospel writers of the New Testament.

This historical order is theologically and interpretively important. The event precedes the faith. Otherwise we are tempted to become ourselves the creators of the gospel, selecting out what we prefer in developing an Easter faith or ethical faith or liberation faith, which is then made the real working center, and once that is established the Gospel records are read backwards from our premise. We then succeed in bringing the Holy Scripture under our own effective control.

Another variation on this methodology is to understand and interpret the New Testament documents too narrowly in terms of the battles and the challenges that the early church confronted in its relationship to Greek and Jewish thought. Rudolf Bultmann has made the most far-reaching interpretive reconstructions by means of this methodology. He has presupposed a fully formed pre-Christian Gnostic source in John's Gospel which for him accounts for much of the emphasis and story-building by John. In addition, he proposes that John's Gospel sifts through Semitic source material as well as certain other sources for several of the event stories about the ministry of Jesus. The mixture of these sources is then recombined by redactors to form the Gospel as we now have it. The result is that the portrayal of Jesus Christ in John's Gospel is the creation of the early Christians as they borrow from Semitic and Gnostic aspirations.

This is how Bultmann explains John's use of the word *logos* in John 1: "It is enough to recognize that the mythological figure of the logos has its home in a particular understanding of the world, namely, the Gnostic. . . . the individual by turning to the Logos, frees himself from the cosmos in order to attain to his Supracosmic home" (Rudolf Bultmann, *Gospel of John*, pp. 24, 25). Bultmann then allows this prior conclusion to carry so much weight in his interpretation that the text in John's Gospel is robbed of its right to speak in its own terms. Ernst Käsemann has challenged Bultmann for this dangerous inversion: "For Bultmann the Easter faith becomes the constant and Jesus the variable."* When this happens, it is the church that has become the real center instead of Jesus Christ himself." Käsemann expresses his concern in even stronger terms: "The cross creates the church and the church represents and does not replace the cross. Nor can the church put itself on the same plane as the cross. It is therefore this note which compels me to oppose Bultmann all along the line and, I am sorry to say, to oppose him in no uncertain terms" (*New Testament Questions of Today*, p. 58). We are not the Gospel nor is John—Jesus Christ and he alone is the Good News.

There is an additional reason why we must not reconstruct the Gospel narratives on the basis of speculations rooted in what we suppose to be the purposes and goals of the first-century church which writes the documents. It is simply a technical fact that documentary evidence of New Testament manuscripts just do not support theories which divide up the Gospel of John into various special interest sources.

Bultmann proposes that the prologue of John comes from the John the Baptist cultic community and is incorporated into the Gospel (*The Gospel of John*, p. 18). But the language and style of the prologue is not so easily separated from the rest of the Gospel, as we have already observed. Added to that is the fact that Bultmann has not been able to find documentary evidences to support the claims for the John the Baptist origin of that material or for the pre-Christian Gnostic material either.

Documentary research also does not support an evolutionary approach to the development of the text of the Gospel of John. We do not find a simple core narrative that is then enlarged through the years by the addition of various stories as the church theoretically needs to support the growing doctrines (e.g., the water-to-wine story to support the growing theology of the Lord's Supper). Instead, there is massive evidence that the text of John as it now stands in the authorized text was composed with literary integrity and in one unified style of writing.

Rudolf Schnackenburg makes the point strongly against the source theories of Bultmann: "Having examined ... the literary

---

*Käsemann puts it this way. "Bultmann expressly adopts as his own H. Braun's statement, 'The constant is the self-understanding of the believer; Christology is the variable'. I hold this judgement to be, quite simply, false and to pick up Bultmann's own distinction, false both historically and materially" (*New Testament Questions of Today*, p. 37).

characteristics of this work, we come to the conclusion that, though not composed in one piece, it testified in the main to the workmanship of one single individual" (*The Gospel According to St. John*, 1:75). The text itself resists, on simply technical textual grounds, the sort of elaborate tracing of trajectories and dogmatic sources which the Bultmannian school of interpretation has developed.

What we have in the Gospel of John, shown dramatically at the wedding in Cana, is that what Jesus says and what he does are an inseparable whole. The eternal word and the concrete event are one; therefore we cannot separate theological truth from the things that Jesus does or from the concrete historical person that Jesus *is*. The New Testament documents refuse to make such a separation. Jesus in the Gospel of John is the Word who becomes flesh. What is love, then, in the Gospel of John? It is the event where Jesus welcomes Andrew and John to spend the day with him to ask their questions; it is Jesus caring about really knowing Nathanael; it is Jesus caring for the embarrassment of a bridegroom at a wedding; it is Jesus, moved deeply by the despair of a city official whose son is dying, healing the son. These are events, and these are what love is in the New Testament. Love in the New Testament is not external theory or concept but the inseparable mixture of word and event. These events are not illustrations of love, they are the very reality itself.

As an interpreter, I would rather struggle with the rough edges and embarrassment of the miracles than try to tame them, to make them less radical and total. I am prepared to take John quite seriously throughout his whole Gospel, to treat his book as a serious faith document that earnestly recounts his recollection of actual events. John's purpose is to stir and encourage our faith, but he shows no signs of historical carelessness.

> Every verse of the gospels tells us that the origin of Christianity is not the Kerygma, not the Resurrection experience of the disciples, not the Christ idea, but an historical event, to wit, the appearance of the man Jesus of Nazareth . . . and his message (Joachim Jeremias, "The Present Position in the Controversy Concerning the Problem of the Historical Jesus," p. 33).

Jesus Christ does not need the church to make his character concrete and exciting. He speaks for himself.

5. The Temple Incident
John 2:12–25

Jesus visits Capernaum with his mother, disciples and brothers. The word here translated "brothers," *adelphoi,* is the common word for blood brother. John gives no names to these brothers, though names are suggested in Matthew 13:55 and Mark 6:3.

One of the contrasts between John's Gospel and Matthew, Mark and Luke is that the Synoptics all concentrate upon the Galilean ministry of Jesus, and most of the ministry recorded by them occurs at or near Capernaum. I believe that John is aware of the other Gospels and his conscious method is ordinarily not to repeat narratives found in them. As we have already noted, John does not record the kind of parables found in Matthew, Mark and Luke; he does not repeat miracle accounts, with the exception of the feeding of the five thousand. His interview accounts are not usually repetitious of the Synoptic accounts. John has very little to say about the Capernaum ministry of Jesus. In this account he mentions the city but immediately moves on to describe the first visit of Jesus to Jerusalem.

John tells us that the passover is at hand, the first of three different passovers during the ministry of Jesus that John will note. In the temple area, Jesus found those who sold sacrificial animals and the moneychangers who exchanged the Roman coins, unacceptable for temple offerings because of the image of Caesar, into half-shekel Tyrian coins which could then be used for the temple tax. These merchants had moved into the temple precincts. Caiaphas as high priest had allowed them to set up their tables in the court of the Gentiles. The sale of animals in the temple area was unprecedented and contrary to the ordinary temple practice, in that if animals got loose they might violate the sanctuary. Research into the first-century period has pointed up that the presence of large numbers of these sacrificial animal merchants and

37

moneychangers stemmed from a controversy between the Sanhedrin and the High Priest Caiaphas (Brown, *Gospel According to
John*, 1:119). Therefore, there is reason to believe that a large
number of rival groups of merchants were in the temple area because of this feud. Caiaphas let in one group of merchants in order
to penalize merchants who had sided with the Sanhedrin against
him.

Jesus enters the temple precinct, and what he now does takes
everyone by surprise. He turns over the tables! Then, as neatly
piled coins are scattered across the pavement, he takes a whip and
forces the traders out of the temple, turning loose the sacrificial
animals to drive them out of the courtyard.

What a startling act! But what is most surprising to the readers
is that no one among either the leaders, the merchants, or the
people makes any move to stop Jesus. The most obvious reason is
that the people approved of his act. Jesus' words may have stirred
the memory of those present to recall the messianic prophecy of
the prophet Zechariah. His final words (Zech. 14:2) tell of the day
of the Lord: "And there shall no longer be a merchant in the house
of the Lord of hosts on that day." John tells us that the disciples
remembered the psalm of David, "Zeal for thy house has consumed
me" (Ps. 69:9). The response of the people who are referred to by
John with the general term "the Jews" is to ask from Jesus what
sign he could show for his act. This is the very question one would
ask of a prophet to ascertain his true credibility.

The fact is, that according to the text, Jesus is not scolded or
threatened for his decisive act. Instead, the act is accepted, perhaps even welcomed, by most of the people, who are perhaps already weary of the chaos caused by the large numbers of tables and
cages that have crowded in upon the temple area. Certainly, the
thoughtful Pharisees would welcome the purification of the
temple. It was Judas Maccabaeus who had purified the temple of
foreign idols in 167 B.C. The memory of that cleansing is commemo-
rated each year in the Feast of Dedication (Hanukkah). Now the
strange Galilean is purifying the temple of the home-grown idols of
avarice and greed. So the people ask for a sign, and the reply of
Jesus is enigmatic and hidden: "Destroy this temple and in three
days I will raise it up." Those who hear these words try to understand them in their most obvious sense. They remind Jesus that
forty-six years have already been spent in the rebuilding of the
great temple.

The temple at Jerusalem has played a very significant role
throughout the history of Israel. It had first been built by Solomon

about 950 B.C. It was destroyed in 586 B.C. by the armies of the Neo-
Babylonian Empire. Seventy years later it was rebuilt on a very
modest scale by Zerubbabel. In 20/19 B.C., Herod the Great began a
major rebuilding which was to result in a temple on a more magnif-
icent scale than even in the time of Solomon. According to Josephus, the project will finally be completed in A.D. 63. This project,
along with other impressive building ventures, gives us some appreciation for the tremendous wealth of the House of Herod.

Jesus has given a sign which is at once both *incomprehensible*
and *unforgettable*. The people do not understand what he really
means, yet they feel uncomfortable and anxious because of what
he says. At the same moment Jesus has given a sign which they will
not forget. In fact his words, twisted out of their original intent
and shape, will be used against him in his trial (Mark 14:58; Matt.
26:61). False witnesses will accuse Jesus of saying he would destroy
the temple. At the cross we have the record of those who mock
Jesus: "You who would destroy the temple and rebuild it . . ."
(Mark 15:29, Matt. 27:40). Also Luke records in Acts 6:14 that at
the trial of Stephen his accusers will claim that Jesus said he
would destroy the temple.

The sign Jesus gives at the temple has touched on a raw nerve.
This, I believe, accounts for the electrifying effect of his words.
The temple is a vital and symbolic national place, and Jesus has
dared to suggest its possible destruction. He has, by the sign, taken
the symbol of the nation's life into his hands. It is very important
to note that in the text Jesus does not make any effort to correct
the misunderstanding of his listeners. He is willing to allow the
sign to stand as it is: he allows the ambiguity to persist. So the sign
shocks the crowd who hear it. It is mysterious by any standard:
How can this man possibly rebuild the temple in three days? The
sign is authoritative. Most of all, the sign has an awesome apocalyptic feel about it. *"Destroy . . . I will* rebuild . . . three *days."*
Only later, after the sign is fulfilled by Christ himself, will it make
sense.

The disciples are no better off than anyone else concerning this
strange saying of Jesus when it comes to understanding its meaning. For them as well as for the others it is totally mysterious and
hidden. The sign becomes a part of the secret messianic sayings of
Jesus. The words bear witness to his messiahship, yet they also
hide that messiahship from the people around him. John concludes this narrative with his own comment concerning the hid-
denness of Jesus: "Jesus did not trust himself to them."

This becomes another instance where Jesus is prepared to take time in making clear who he is and what his ministry means. He is willing to allow great signposts to stand along the path which apparently do not seem of any help to the journeyers, except that Jesus himself is the one who grants the sign.

There is a technical question we must still ask. How are we to reconcile the timing of the temple incidents between John and the Synoptic Gospels? The Synoptic accounts place the cleansing of the temple following the Palm Sunday entry into Jerusalem, while John records this event near the beginning of Christ's ministry. Those interpreters who argue against John's positioning feel it improbable that such an affront against the temple would go unchallenged by the authorities. These arguments (C. H. Dodd, C. K. Barrett) are not so convincing to me. The evidence of the account is that what Jesus *does* is not rejected by the people, but welcomed. There is, I believe, a parallel to John the Baptist who, though he has a stern and judgmental message, is nevertheless popular with the people. It is not at all improbable that Jesus' act in the temple was welcomed by many of the people at large, and perhaps even members of the Pharisee party—which could help us to understand the Nicodemus interview of the next chapter. Remember that Nicodemus comments upon the signs that Jesus does.

There are other commentators who favor John's placement as preferred to the Synoptic accounts (J. A. T. Robinson, La Grange). Another hypothesis (see B. F. Westcott, *The Gospel According to St. John*) is that Jesus on *two* occasions confronted the money-changers and salesmen in the temple, once at the beginning of his ministry, and a second time after his triumphal entry into Jerusalem. This option is not improbable. It fits with what we know of the tenaciousness of human sinfulness that not long after Jesus himself left the temple the tables were set up again. This view makes the most sense to me.

The really important thing that happened at Jerusalem during this first visit is that by what Jesus *does* and *says* a signpost has been planted in Jerusalem. The sign is clear about one thing, and that is the mysterious authority of Christ—"I will build up." But its deeper, richer meaning will remain hidden until the death and resurrection of Jesus Christ. It is something like the strange lamppost which the first visitors in Narnia find in the Winter Kingdom in C. S. Lewis's *The Lion, the Witch and the Wardrobe*. It is not until much later that the meaning of the lamppost becomes clear. Nevertheless it plays a part in the story. It sheds a strange and real light and helps the journeyers to find their way.

So it is with the signs of Jesus in the Gospel records. Each signpost along the way has meaning within itself and at the same moment points beyond itself. In no instance is one of the signs perfectly clear or complete; in each case it is helpful yet disturbing, illuminating and confusing all at the same time. The signs fulfill expectations and disappoint them. But the reason for this is that the Lord to whom they point is himself noncapturable, by either his friends or his foes.

6. Encounter with a Pharisee
John 3:1-21

John now introduces us to Nicodemus who is a Pharisee and a member of the Sanhedrin. The Sanhedrin is a council made up of seventy men. The High Priest is its chairman and the members come from the priesthood, the scribes and other elders from the aristocracy. This body is usually dominated by the Sadducee Party (the priestly movement that traces its origins all the way back to Zadok, 1 Kings 1:32), though the Pharisees are also represented. Later in the history of Judaism the Pharisees will win control of this important body.

The Pharisee movement has a very important influence upon the life of Israel and will be the principle spiritual and intellectual force in Judaism following the destruction of Jerusalem in A.D. 70. The Pharisees have their beginnings as a movement at the time of the Syrian occupation of Judah almost two hundred years before Christ. Their roots go to the *Hasidim,* the "godly people" who were faithful to the worship of the God of Israel in the face of the idolatrous influences of the Syrian occupation. At first they supported the house of the Maccabees in their leadership of the revolt against Syria, but later, after the success of the revolt when the Maccabeans (also called, the Hasmonaean House) turned corrupt with success, the Hasidim separated from the Hasmonaens. As a result a new name is coined for them: they are the separatists, "perusim," hence *Pharisees.*

These earnest separatists are a lay movement, and throughout most of their history they see themselves over against the priesthood, almost all of whom are Sadducees. The Pharisees are well educated, deeply concerned about the traditions of Israel and the preservation of those traditions. "In the course of their study of the law they built upon a body of traditional interpretations and application of the law which in due course tended to assume a

42

validity as sacrosanct as that of the written Law itself" (F. F. Bruce, *New Testament History*, p. 69). It is estimated that at the time of Jesus there are approximately seven thousand members of this lay movement. They have very great influence with the people at large, due to their knowledge of both the law and the traditions, and also because of their admirable ethical goals. Many Pharisees fast twice a week and give the money thus saved to the poor. They are intellectuals; they are socially concerned moderates. The aristocracy is Sadducee, and the angry and disillusioned are either the "drop out" Essenes, who live in almost absolute separation at Qumran, or the fierce Zealots who, because of their terrorism, are eventually, according to Josephus, the provocative cause of the tragedy of the A.D. 70 destruction of Jerusalem by the Romans.

But in the New Testament Gospels, the Pharisees are the ones we meet more than the others. They are most interested in the teachings of Jesus; they take the trouble of traveling to the northern village of Capernaum to hear what Jesus has to say (see Luke 5). Jesus also takes them seriously. We have the record of numerous conversations in the New Testament between the Pharisees and Jesus, whereas there are only a handful of recorded dialogue scenes between Jesus and members of the Sadducee party.

Like any movement that has developed elaborate special doctrines, the Pharisees have become defensive and very protective with reference to those specialized doctrines. This tense defensiveness becomes clear in the running objection that the Pharisees have toward Jesus in regard to the correct observance of the Sabbath. Their special rules have gone far beyond the words of the Law of Moses concerning the Sabbath, and in fact are so complex that the aid of highly trained lawyers is necessary to know how to apply them. What makes matters still more complicated is that the Essenes at Qumram have gone even farther than the Pharisees in their interpretations and requirements. Their Sabbath Laws are even more exacting and difficult to follow. Jesus is aware of this difference between Essenes and Pharisees when he asks the question of a group of Pharisees, "If your donkey were to fall into the ditch on the Sabbath, would you aid the donkey?" The point is that the Pharisees had not covered that possibility but the Essenes had. By such a question Jesus dares to challenge the legalistic trivialization into which such tradition-building had inevitably led.

But what is most important for us to understand in trying to make sense of the Pharisees is that fundamental to these laymen is a much larger quest than their technical worries over Sabbath observance. These people are serious about knowing the will of God, and they really care about the truth, but they have become proud and self-righteous like anyone who develops a degree of expertise in such a quest. The result is that they are hypocritical and contemptuous toward ordinary people. Though more moderate than the Essenes at Qumram, nevertheless they show little mercy toward "sinners" and enemies. It is clear, therefore, that the Pharisees are a complicated mixture of people, and it is important for interpreters of the New Testament accounts to keep this fact in mind.

Now we come to Nicodemus. He has not come to Jesus in order to debate card-playing, social dancing, and movies—the minutiae of the Law. John shows us from Nicodemus' first sentence that this Pharisee is undertaking a quest into the sources and origins behind tradition. He comes "by night." This phrase may imply Nicodemus' fear of being identified with Jesus. Or an equally plausible interpretation is, perhaps, his desire to have an in-depth, uninterrupted conversation. Nicodemus pays tribute to Jesus as a teacher come from God because of the "signs." Has Nicodemus heard about events that have occurred in Galilee? Is he impressed by the temple incident? We do not know.

The answer that Jesus gives, though John may have compressed the full dialogue, is sudden and goes to the heart of Nicodemus' deepest quest. "Unless one is born from above [again] he can not see the kingdom of God."

This is a remarkable answer. It shows that Jesus rightly understands the fundamental longing behind the tradition of the Pharisees. They longed for the kingly reign of Yahweh. Even the most technically obscure legalist would feel in his heart that the reason for each tradition was to glorify God and therefore in some small way prepare for and welcome the kingdom. The word *kingdom,* which is so extensively used in the Synoptics, does not appear elsewhere in John's Gospel apart from this scene. But its use here is very decisive. Jesus makes it clear to Nicodemus that a new beginning from above is needed to experience God's kingdom.

The Greek word translated "from above" is the word *anothen,* which may mean both "again" and "from above." It is this built-in ambiguity in the Greek word that Nicodemus takes advantage of to pose a question to Jesus. "How ... can he enter a *second time* into his mother's womb ... ?" Since this ambiguity is not present in either Hebrew or Aramaic (see Brown, *Gospel According to John,* p. 130) this provides for us an interior clue to the fact that Jesus probably carried on his teaching in the Greek language.

The Lord replies that Nicodemus must be *born of water* and the *Spirit*. The word for water in this dialogue is not theologically defined by Jesus. We are not certain what is meant by his use of the word. Is it a reference to the baptism of repentance or to an act of faith? The word *Spirit* is defined by its use. In both Greek and Hebrew, the word for spirit is literally the word for wind; *ruach* in Hebrew, *pneuma* in Greek. Jesus says that the wind blows where it wills. The divine authority of God is affirmed. He is the one who decides upon whom the wind should blow. We experience the wind, but we do not limit or control it. With this analogy the authority of God as the one who invites men and women into his own kingdom is preserved by Jesus. Though there are profound mysteries within the analogy, the one point that is made very clear is the kingly authority of God.

Nicodemus asks a final question that is in effect a sigh: "How can this be?" What is the force of that question? It is really, I believe, the dual question, "Who can this be for?" and "Why is this so?" Certainly Jesus by his reply answers those two great and all-important questions. By the Old Testament illustration from Numbers 21:9, Jesus makes it clear that the wind of God is a *redemptive* wind. His kingdom is the kingdom of salvation for those gravely in need. It is in this setting that Jesus gives to his listener a new sign concerning himself. "As Moses lifted . . . so must the Son of man be lifted. . . ." As the sign given at the temple in chapter 2 is hidden, so this one, though impossible to forget, is also hard to understand. Only later will its meaning become clear. The words that follow this Old Testament sign are less hidden.

The speech of Jesus continues. (I hold that verses 16-21 are the completion of the speech of Jesus to Nicodemus and are not John's reflection upon the event.) He goes on to make clear his reply to the deepest questions that Nicodemus has posed—"for whom?" and "why?" The most memorable verse in all of the New Testament appears in this context: "For God so loved the world that he gave his only Son, that whoever believes in him should not perish but have everlasting life."

This amazing sentence and the sentences that follow (vv. 17-21) answer the *why* question, the *for whom* question and the *how* question:

1. *Why.* Jesus gives a twofold answer to this question. The illustration of the children of Israel and Moses makes the point that in the face of the people's peril, God at that time provided a means of help. Nicodemus' generation and its peril is linked by Jesus to Moses' generation. As a few people in the desert were helped by

the act of God in that early age, so now there is provided, on a profoundly wider scale, help for the peril of the whole world. The
point is clear—as Moses' age was in need of help, so Nicodemus
and his age are in the same need. The issue now, as then, is life or
death. Therefore it is the need of humanity that becomes one part
of the answer to the question, *why is this so?*

But the reason that receives even more attention by Jesus is the
divine motivation that stands behind God's mighty act. God so
loved the world that he spoke for himself: he made himself known
as mankind's only redeemer.

God's decision stands before and prior to every other fact; even
the crisis in which humanity is perishing comes in the middle of
this great sentence, not at its beginning. Only the love of God is at
the beginning. Jesus has defined *love* in the same way that *Spirit*
was earlier defined—by its usage in the sentence. Love is the event
Jesus Christ; love is Jesus Christ granting life; love sets free from
death and condemnation; love creates the possibility of faith.

We need to hear this in our own generation. So often we are
tempted to teach about God's love as if it were the afterthought,
the kindly response of God to our crisis. There is an arrogance in
that sequence which has poisoned much of our theology. When the
World Council of Churches was convened for its first Assembly in
Amsterdam in 1946, the title for that Assembly was "Man's Disorder and God's Design." It was the evangelical theologian Karl
Barth who dared to challenge the arrogance of the title in his historic address at the Assembly. He argued that if we are to be faithful to the Bible, we cannot consider man's disorder until we have
discovered God's will. Therefore the title should read "God's Design and Man's Disorder."

2. The *for whom* question is answered by the use of sweeping,
universal language—*the world, whoever.* The conversation with
Nicodemus begins with the traditions of Israel, the illustration
taken from the exodus experiences of the chosen people, and then
moves toward the universal implications of those ancient traditions for all of humanity.

3. The question *how* moves in two directions. The first direction
is theological, *Godward;* the second is existential, toward us who
are men and women. How does God bring aid? By the hidden sign
of Moses in the wilderness we discover the strange new way. In this
conversation with Nicodemus, Jesus continues to build a theology
of the cross. The theology was introduced by John the Baptist in
his phrase *lamb of God.* It was enlarged by Jesus in the sign of the
temple given at Jerusalem, and is now by the sign of Moses in the

wilderness. We only know in a hidden sense that Jesus has been *given* by God the Father in our behalf. Finally, in answer to the question *how*, Jesus tells of faith—"whoever believes." Belief is defined in the passage as the welcoming of truth; a conscious human move toward the Son of God.

The encounter with Nicodemus is left without a conclusion, though later in the Gospel the writer will speak once more about this ruler of the Jews. What Nicodemus has heard from Jesus must have been both disappointing and fulfilling. He has heard the hard words that, though experienced and well traveled, he must begin again in his lifelong search for the kingdom of God. Jesus has called Nicodemus to a radically new pathway, and such a claim as this must be disappointing to someone who has successfully achieved, through his Pharisaism, public respect and honor. Now all of these achievements are overruled by the *good news* of Jesus. The special interests of Nicodemus in the technicalities of Sabbath observance are not even mentioned by Jesus. But at the same moment, what Nicodemus has discovered must be very encouraging to this earnest man. Jesus has assured him that indeed there is the kingdom, and more than that, that the kingdom of God is for him; and even more, that it has universal relevance for all mankind. Now Nicodemus himself must decide.

". . . here we are standing at the centre. And however high and mysterious and difficult everything we want to know might seem to us, yet we may also say that this is just where everything becomes quite simple, quite straightforward, quite childlike. Right here in this centre, in which as a Professor of Systematic Theology I must call to you, 'Look! This is the point now! Either knowledge, or the greatest folly!' Here I am in front of you, like a teacher in Sunday School facing his kiddies, who has something to say which a mere four-year-old can really understand. 'The world was lost, but Christ was born, rejoice . . .' " (Barth, *Dogmatics in Outline,* pp. 66, 67).

7. *Friend of the Bridegroom*
John 3:22–36

This passage poses certain problems for interpretation. As we have already noted, John's method is to make his own comments about events in the narrative. The marriage at Cana incident is concluded with just such a theological comment: "This, the first of his signs, Jesus did at Cana . . . and manifested his glory." The problem for the English translator and interpreter is that in the original Greek manuscripts there are no markings that indicate quotation marks, such as we have in English. This means that the translator and interpreter must decide where quotation is taking place on the basis of the context of the sentences themselves. As a result, there are several places, especially in John's Gospel, where a decision must be made by the reader. We noted this in the dialogue with Nicodemus. In this present text we must make a similar judgment. John the Baptist is clearly the speaker in verses 27–30. But what shall we do with verses 31–36? The RSV translators have rendered this section as the comment by the writer John. Other interpreters, such as Brown, Schnackenburg, and Bultmann, see the paragraph as the words of Jesus. Some of these would move the paragraph so that it follows the Nicodemus dialogue. Others, such as Barrett and Calvin, feel that the paragraph is the continuation of the speech of John the Baptist. I find this third position to be the most persuasive.

The text begins as John tells us that Jesus and his disciples went out from Jerusalem into the territory of Judah. The previous scene takes place in Jerusalem, which of course is in Judea; therefore John's point must be that they leave the city for the countryside of the province. We are then told that Jesus and his disciples baptized. (Jesus did not himself baptize. See 4:2.) John tells us that John the Baptist was then at Aenon near Salim. This is probably the site in Samaria near Shechem. There were springs in this area,

48

a fact which explains the reference, "there was much water there." In this sentence John's Gospel shows a concern for details which we now want to consider.

How good a geographer and technical historian is John? Opinion regarding this issue has gone through an interesting cycle in that regard. By the early part of the twentieth century, in many circles of New Testament interpretation the Gospel of John was not seriously looked to as a source of reliable data concerning the actual history of Jesus' ministry. The book had, instead, been interpreted by many of the form critics of that day as a second-century theological dogmatic portrayal of the Christ of faith. Therefore, to them the book had very little historical value except to provide insight into the theology of the primitive church. "... in the early years of this century, scholarship went through a period of extreme skepticism about this Gospel. John was dated very late, even to the second half of the Second Century. As a product of the Hellenistic World, it was thought to be totally devoid of historical value, and to have little relation to the Palestine of Jesus of Nazareth" (Brown, *Gospel According to John*, 1:xxi).

Rudolf Bultmann brought the Gospel of John to the center of New Testament scholarly concerns by the publication of his commentary in 1941. His commentary was bold and new. The liberal scholarship of the late nineteenth and twentieth centuries had been embarrassed by the vast and intimate Christ in John, since they preferred the milder, ethical advice of the good teacher Jesus that Protestant liberalism had created. We owe a debt to Bultmann for his journey out of the wasteland that characterized liberalism's New Testament studies. But in my view, his journey was only half done. He found the vital importance of the wholly transcendent in Easter faith, but he celebrated that faith unto itself, whereas it is the historical Jesus of Nazareth who is the true source; and the wonder that he as Living Lord can be known is the real celebration. There is a vital connection between the Jesus of history and the Easter faith that Jesus created by his victory over death, sin and the devil. It is this vital connection that Bultmann missed. Nevertheless, his 1941 commentary had achieved the important task of reopening the subject of Johannine studies in a new and dramatic way.

Since 1941 many discoveries have been made about the background of the New Testament: the Dead Sea Scrolls, the Gnostic library at Nag Hammadi Egypt, and the very recent Syrian excavations at Ebla. These sets of documents have helped to settle linguistic questions and have established in different ways the linguistic unity of John's Gospel. We have been able to see the independence of John from both the Gnostics and the Essenes. "Perhaps the most important service of the Dead Sea Scrolls will be the demonstration which may be brought from them that John the synoptics, St. Paul . . . draw from a common reservoir of terminology and ideas which were well known to the Essenes, and presumably familiar also to other Jewish sects of the period" (W. F. Albright, "Recent Discoveries," p. 169). Dr. Albright goes on, with examples, to establish the sharp cleavage in outlook between John's Gospel and the teaching of the Essenes (see pp. 170 ff.). The recent work done by archeologists has given John high marks for technical accuracy as an historian. The reference in this text to Aenon near Salim is a case in point. Critics of the old school had tended to discount the historical value of this geographical description, choosing instead to treat the place symbolically and as fiction, *springs* (aenon) near peace, salvation (Salim). But the place is real and moreover John's description is accurate (see Brown, *Gospel According to John,* p. 151). The archeologist L. H. Vincent confirms that John's naming of the Roman pavement (John 19) as *Gabbatha* is another instance of his precise and accurate understanding of the landmarks of Jerusalem. (See Albright, "Recent Discoveries," p. 158.) John is accurate in the location of Jacob's well in chapter 4. His naming of the well as Bethesda in chapter 5 is correct, and is confirmed by the Copper Scroll of the Dea Sea Scrolls discovery. Brown issues a warning to interpreters who have too quickly dismissed John's historical data: "scholars have become more cautious now that some Johannine place names, once accounted to be purely symbolic (e.g., Bethesda) have been shown to be factual" (*Gospel According to John, p. 45*).

In John 3:25–36 we have the final speech of John the Baptist to appear in this Gospel. These are not really new affirmations. They have already been spoken in one way or another by John the Baptist. But they come in the setting of dialogue and controversy. He describes himself as the bridegroom's friend. He has experienced the fulfillment of his own life in welcoming the one who is to be the central figure.

The most fascinating feature of the dialogue is that, though the conversation begins with discussion about baptisms and rites of purification, John the Baptist shows little interest in those questions. This is remarkable in light of the fact that he has been primarily associated in the minds of the people as one who advocates a unique baptism. We know from the Dead Sea Scrolls that the issue of washings and rites of purification are in fact very major questions among groups in that period. But John the Baptist breaks away from that advocacy to which he has given so much of his life, to center his attention on the larger question—the greater matter. He moves the conversation to the question that is most central and upon which every other question depends: *Has God spoken for himself in Jesus Christ?* This is the christological question, the fundamental issue for all theology. John the Baptist is the first systematic theologian of Christendom. He has rightly discerned that the discussions about various baptisms and advocacies, of which there were many in the first century as there are in our century, are of secondary importance until we have decided who Jesus Christ is. It hasn't changed since then. "Tell me how it stands with your Christology, and I'll tell you who you are" (Karl Barth, *Dogmatics in Outline*, p. 66).

Jesus breaks through ancient barriers to find a human being in need.

8. The Samaritans
John 4:1-42

Jesus and his disciples are en route from Judea north to Galilee. One of the possible routes north, though not the one usually used by travelers, is through Samaria.

Who are the Samaritans? The Samaritans of the first century are descendants of two groups: first, those not deported or killed in the fall of the Northern Kingdom in 722 B.C.; second, foreign colonists brought in from Babylonia by the Assyrian conquerors who, by their intermarriage, became a part of the heritage of the Samaritans. Today this ancient people still exist in two settlements in what is modern Israel and now number some five thousand in total population.

The town near Jacob's well at which Jesus and his disciples stop for a rest is probably ancient Shechem, which came into the Greek text as Sychar. While the disciples are in the city, Jesus requests the favor of a drink of water from the lone other person at the well —a Samaritan woman. The woman's response is her reminder to Jesus that Jews and Samaritans have no dealings. This real enmity goes back to the Syrian occupation of Judea when the Samaritans had intermarried with the Syrians. In addition, during the Jewish uprising under the leadership of the Maccabean brothers, the Samaritans had sided with the Syrians. Added to this there are the theological differences between Jews and Samaritans on the nature and content of parts of the Old Testament Law and Writings. The Samaritans do not accept the prophetic writings, and their Pentateuch has different textual readings than the Hebrew Pentateuch. By the time of the first century there is very minimal relationship between these two nations, who are nevertheless both children of Abraham. Now we can appreciate the surprise element that is present at the very opening of this incident.

The reply of Jesus is to offer to this woman by the well "living water." She is intrigued by his strange offer but does not understand how his promise works or where the water is from. Then Jesus enlarges the living water teaching; it is to be a "water welling up to eternal life." She immediately responds in the affirmative to that offer.

The next sequence in the dialogue is at first embarrassing to the woman but is in fact an essential part of the encounter because of her needs and because of the very nature of Jesus Christ. It can be cruelty at its meanest to confront people with their problems, their hidden defeats and sorrows, unless there is a way through those problems. Here is a person who has a history of broken human relationships, and her lonely journey to draw water at noontime may itself signal the rejection that she has experienced from the women in her city. The question is, why does Jesus now by his question and comment confront her with this added reminder of her moral crisis? The difference is that it is Jesus who has posed the crisis, and we recognize in this encounter the salty side of the gospel. There is the joyous fulfillment side represented by the open and free offer of living water, and then in the next moment the realistic encounter with the whole self of a person in profound crisis.

Both ingredients are mixed together in John's portrayal of the ministry of Jesus Christ. The celebrative water-to-wine incident in chapter 2 is immediately followed by the salty confrontation in the temple at Jerusalem. In chapter 3, Nicodemus hears the joyous news that there is indeed the kingdom of God for which he has searched his whole life, *but* he must start over again at a new beginning point and be born again, which stings a proud man who has worked so hard for so long a time. Now the woman at the well is offered living water. The image of water is not really explained by Jesus, except to equate it with eternal life, and though she may not fully understand all of the mystery involved in its meaning, she is strongly drawn to its inviting promise—*whatever it is, it is good!* But the joy is immediately clouded with the reality of who she is and the unfolding by Jesus of his awareness of her story, a story of interpersonal defeats and disappointments.

But we must see here, theologically, that the vivid clarification of who this Samaritan woman really is, is not an interruption in an otherwise kindly dialogue. This very disclosure is the love of Jesus Christ breaking through a painful barrier in order to find one lonely human being. That search is the Good News. Notice how powerfully and helpfully Jesus is able to move in close to our real selves. The ancient barriers of nation and religion and tradition do not keep him out.

(1) Jesus breaks through the racist barrier. (2) He breaks through the sexist barrier (rabbis do not ordinarily speak openly with women in public v. 27). (See Brown, *Gospel According to John*, p. 173.) (3) He breaks through the masks which hide our painful and sensitive feelings about who we are. In T. S. Eliot's poem, "The Love Song of J. Alfred Prufrock," we meet a wistful man who has succeeded in hiding himself throughout his whole life. He always puts on "a face to meet the faces that you meet." At the heart of Eliot's classic appraisal of twentieth-century Western man/woman is the mixture of the fear of being found out and the aching desire to be truly found.

What happens by the well is that this one human being is both found out and found by Jesus Christ. There cannot really be good news that means life to the real me without both this finding and the finding out. Now the Samaritan woman knows that the joyous living water has been offered to the real person behind the mask. The fact that Jesus truly understands who she is has heightened the richness of the gift of life to her. The impact is profound. Later in this chapter she will tell the people in her village, "Come see a man who told me all that I ever did." As with Nathanael, who was won by being deeply found, so this person is won as she is found by Jesus Christ.

In the discussion with the Samaritan woman, Jesus accepts the importance of the Jews as the people from whom salvation comes to the world, but at the same moment he speaks in nonnationalistic terms of the fact that the true worshipers will worship God in spirit and in truth. In each instance, Jesus uses a name for God which is new to the ears of the first-century Jews and Samaritans. It is the word *father*. By the time of the first century, the holy names for God had been suppressed from use by the pious. It was judged that to use God's holy name would amount to a violation of the third commandment. Therefore oblique terms and phrases were developed to refer to God. This was especially true of the most holy name for God, *Yahweh*. Jesus and the New Testament writers make a dramatic break with this traditional reticence. The great "I am" passages in the Gospel of John represent our Lord's direct identification of himself with Yahweh. In literal terms, the name Yahweh is the third person singular of the Hebrew verb "to be."

Now Jesus makes use of the most intimate word available to describe God—*Father*. In this text we are taught by Jesus that God is honored not by religious avoidance of his name but by faith in him "in spirit and in truth." Jesus has shifted the direction of the

question about the places where the worship of God is preferred to
the prior relationship that is fundamental to all worship—the relationship between the believer and God. The Samaritans to this day
attach primary respect and affection for Mt. Gerizim near
Shechem. In fact, in the Samaritan Bible, Deuteronomy 27:4 records that Joshua was told to set up a shrine on Gerizim and not,
as in the reading in the Hebrew Bible, on Mt. Ebal.

The incident closes with the disciples' bafflement at what has
taken place. What is it that has confused them? They have gone to
the city for food and now, on their return, their teacher seems preoccupied. He shows no interest in the noon meal they have
brought. What had begun for them as an everyday task has been
reinterpreted by Jesus into something bigger. Jesus speaks to them
about the universal goals of God and he demonstrates that very
universality. This radical enlargement of a common event is bound
to have an unsettling effect upon the disciples; it still does twenty
centuries later. Added to this is the surprise of all their traditional
feelings about conversations with Samaritans and women! No one
is ever really prepared for the implications of the universal relevance of Jesus Christ.

Through the Samaritan city's response to him, Jesus uses the
image of the harvest to teach his disciples that they are to be reap-
ers of a great harvest which they did not plant. John pays tribute
to the powerful effect of the witness of one human being to Jesus.
Up to this point in the Gospel, the two most persuasive witnesses
to Christ have been John the Baptist and this Samaritan woman
by the well. She begins a new era of preachers of the gospel. What
is deeply impressive is that she is a Samaritan, a woman, and an
outsider. One by one, as this Gospel of Jesus and his ministry unfolds, the expectations we brought to the gospel are being wonder-
fully challenged by the Lord of the gospel.

We see people in a village respond warmly to Jesus Christ in
defiance of over one hundred and fifty years of smoldering resentment against the Jews. Jesus, though he is a Jew, has won their affection. This universal relevance of Jesus that begins here so dramatically will continue to spread beyond the borders of Palestine
to encircle the earth.

Jesus also confirms the gospel perspective concerning the meaning and worth of persons as persons. What is so profoundly important in the encounter with the Samaritan woman is just that. She
was related to as a unique person who was important as a unique
person. She is not lumped into some traditional category but as a
human being is honored by the full and individual attention of

Jesus Christ. She is taken seriously, which of course is why the Lord must grapple with her unique crisis. In no way is she as a woman discounted by Jesus.

In the Nag Hammadi discoveries in Egypt of second-century Gnostic sources, we see a far different picture than this. Note the sexism revealed in the following quotation from the Gospel of Thomas (A. Guillaumont, et al., *The Gospel According to Thomas*, p. 57). "Simon Peter said to them: Let Mary go out from among us, because women are not worthy of life. Jesus said: 'See, I shall lead her, so that I will make her male, that she too may become a living spirit, resembling you males. For every woman who makes herself male will enter the kingdom of Heaven.' " In this document the Gnostics reveal a fundamental rejection of femaleness. But Jesus Christ in no way remolds the woman by the well into anything other than who she is as a Samaritan woman—unique and beloved —except that he sets her free from bondage to sin and calls her to the way of discipleship. What this means for us is that in discovering Christ as Lord, we as persons are not blurred or cancelled so that our race, age, or sex has from that moment no further importance or significance. Rather it is our experience that we find ourselves more than ever. We become who we truly are.

9. A Man from Capernaum
John 4:43-54

This passage begins with a transitional paragraph telling of
Jesus' journey back to the region of Galilee. Verse 44 is a one-
sentence remark by John that of itself does not make sense apart
from an awareness of Luke's Nazareth account (Luke 4). John has
given us no hint of any resistance to Jesus in his hometown of Nazareth. Sentences like this one give us evidence to support the hypothesis that the writer of this Gospel is aware of the other Gospels and that they are being circulated among the churches. He
expects that his readers have had the opportunity to read the
other accounts. This supports the view that the Gospel accounts
were in fact circulated in the early church. Luke by his preface
(Luke 1: 1–4) has also provided us with such evidence.

John records an incident at Cana that offers still another portrayal of Jesus Christ and the people who seek him out. The dialogue brings to the reader a new ingredient in the unfolding self-
disclosure of Jesus. A royal official from Capernaum asks Jesus to
come to Capernaum in order to heal his son who is near death.

Who is this man? The term *basilikos* is used to designate a royal
official: either of the house of Herod or a Roman official. Interpreters have for a long time identified this man with the centurion in
Matthew 8:5–13, Luke 7:1–10. If we were to take this line of reasoning, we have then in John's account a portrait of an event that
is recorded in Matthew and Luke but with some differences in details. Luke tells of a centurion whose "slave" *(doulos)* was sick,
Matthew tell of a sick "servant" *(pais)*—a word that means boy,
both in the sense of "son" and in the sense of "servant boy, slave."
In his account John has made changes in the earlier narratives of
Matthew and Luke. If indeed John is referring to the same incident, then these changes show John's willingness to clarify and
also, if necessary, to correct the other Gospel writers on questions

57

of detail. John tells us that it is the official's *son*, not his servant, who was ill and he makes the point clear that the dialogue is between Jesus and the official directly, whereas Luke and Matthew do not agree on that point. In Matthew it is the centurion who speaks to Jesus; in Luke there are messengers who represent the centurion.

At other times in his Gospel, John will give us details and corrections, so that we conclude that this is one of his purposes in writing.

I am impressed by this example of the concern for accuracy which we observe in the four Gospels. Writers have recorded events as they witnessed them or heard of them. One important clue to the historical credibility of a total document like the New Testament is just this kind of ragged edges between accounts concerning details. The result is that the reader has more confidence in the actual historical reality of an event because of the differences that show up in the narrative records. The fact is that we have a startling, exciting and true event. It happened! The witnesses do not fully agree on certain of the details, but none of them has missed the main, amazing point of the event. The shock of the way Christ's love broke through and was accepted, simply because he said it, made a profound impression that none of the writers missed. Any student of trial law knows that three witnesses to an event who tell identical accounts of that incident are immediately suspect. What we have in the New Testament Gospels are writers who honestly record events as they heard of them or saw them. The mark of earnest concern for truthfulness is present on every page of the New Testament books. If this incident is the same occasion as recorded in Matthew and Luke, then we may observe that that earnestness causes John to correct the record of Matthew and Luke principally at two points simply because he wrote truthfully.

This robust historical honesty provides us with another technical and scholarly reason for confidence in the New Testament.

The first response of Jesus to the official is apparently negative. He does not say no to the man's questions but he does not say yes. Jesus speaks in general terms: "Unless you see signs and wonders you will not believe." This is a surprising sentence. It was Jesus who first gave signs to the disciples and to the people (John 2: 1–11); is he now indicating a shift away from signs and wonders to some other basis for the faith of the disciples? At the heart of this rebuke from Jesus is his intent to develop in the disciples a ground for certitude that will need signs and wonders less and less as the basis for faith.

The question we must ask for this new teaching is—what then shall be the basis of faith for the disciples if it is not to be a continuous demonstration of signs? The Capernaum official, in his great personal anguish and by his response, becomes our teacher. Though Jesus has apparently rejected the official's appeal with a response which seems to imply a termination of the signs, nevertheless the man holds on to the character of Jesus and brings his need to Jesus simply and directly: "Sir, come down before my child dies." Jesus answers, "Go; your son will live." The man from Capernaum believes what Jesus says to him. He believes the word of Jesus without signs. He believes on the basis of the character of Jesus Christ. Later on, when the news of his son's recovery is brought to him, he experiences the joy of the sign, but now in the very confluence of hope and despair, this foreign soldier takes Jesus at his word. He simply trusts Jesus.

His faith has three main ingredient parts that we are able to observe in this account: (1) His faith in Christ begins out of a deep interior awareness of grave need. He has sought out the help of Jesus because of that need. Throughout their encounter, the sharp reality of that need is intensified by the delay and by the first words of Jesus which sound as if the Lord is refusing to act in the face of this one man's human need. This man has been faced with a roadblock. There is a certain similarity in this roadblock to the question Jesus spoke to the woman at the well, "Go call your husband, and come here."

(2) The official's response to that roadblock is nevertheless to stay with Jesus and to bring before the Lord the only credential he has apart from his faith—a very sick son. In chapter 6 of the Gospel Jesus will again place a hard barrier across the pathway of faith by some very difficult teaching about his own total centrality as the bread of life. In that instance John will tell us that many disciples will no longer follow him. But here in Cana this man from Capernaum is different. He does not argue about the words of Jesus; he does not walk away in despair; he does not seek out another healer; he simply and persistently claims the love of Jesus Christ. This claim upon who Christ is, his very nature, is Christian faith.

(3) The second test to the faith of the official follows the words of Jesus. Jesus does not come down to Capernaum as he was requested but instead assures the man that his son will live. Will this be enough? Jesus speaks and this man believes him. He trusts the character of Jesus and acts upon the integrity of that character. The sign comes later.

By the Bethesda Pool Jesus confronts the timeless problem of
depression and despair.

10. The Lonely One
John 5:1–15

This account tells of the second visit of Jesus to Jerusalem. The time is not given to us in this case, except by the indefinite comment that there was "a feast." Perhaps this is the Feast of Weeks —we cannot be certain.

John tells of the pool in Jerusalem, near the sheep gate, called "Bethesda" in Hebrew. John's specific geographical notation has been recently validated from two sources. The copper scroll found at Qumram has named the pool on the eastern hill in Jerusalem as "Bet 'Esda," "house of the flowing" (J. T. Milik, *Discoveries in the Judean Desert* 3(1962):71; see also Brown's *Gospel According to John,* pp. 206–7). Added to this, archeologists have successfully excavated the pool site and have found its five porticoes as John described them.

There is a textual problem in this narrative concerning verse 4, which the RSV has placed into the footnote due to its lack of support in the major New Testament manuscripts: "For an angel of the Lord went down at certain seasons into the pool, and troubled the water; whoever stepped in first after the troubling of the water was healed of whatever disease he had." There is more support for the phrase at the end of verse 3 "waiting for the moving of the water." Seven non-Johannine words appear in verse 4, and it appears, therefore, to be an addition to the original text, perhaps made by an ancient scribe to clarify the scene. Even without verse 4 we are able to conclude its main point from verse 7.

In this incident Jesus initiates dialogue with a man who had been by the Bethesda pool for a long time and had been sick for thirty-eight years. Jesus asks the question, "Do you want to be healed?" This man does not hear Jesus' question, which only needed a simple yes or no answer. Instead, he tells the lonely story of his disappointment with the pool, because when the water was bubbling he never had the chance to get into the water; others were always in before him.

Here is a portrait of a depressed and totally discouraged person. He is so completely captive to his negative feelings about his situation that he is unable even to hear a new question. His answer sounds more like an explanation that he had perhaps given over and over again. The man answers as if Jesus had asked the question, "Why are you here?" Had he talked before to the committee from the Parks and Recreation department or students from the University of Jerusalem writing reports on current health hazards of the pool? His answer is a complaint about the injustice of the system which has all these years kept him from entering the pool.

If Jesus had not interrupted the conversation, this man's next sentences might have urged that Jesus and his committee work toward a new numbering system, so that people like him who have no friends might have a chance at the pool when its waters are troubled. But Jesus interrupts his lonely spiral of self-pity and hopelessness with the sharp command: "Stand up, pick up your mat and walk around." Immediately, John tells us, the man got up and carried away his bed, as Jesus had told him to do.

This incident portrays the authority and love of Jesus in a setting different from what we have observed to this point. Here no request is made of Jesus, and for that matter no real dialogue takes place. A little later in the passage we discover that the sick man does not even know who Jesus is. The account records, instead, the direct intervention of Jesus in the life of a man who is so completely dulled by disappointment that he cannot even respond to a simple question about possible help.

What a contrast between this man and the official from Capernaum. The contrast shows that it takes more emotional strength to ask for help than to tell about the impossibility of help. A human being may be so fatigued and emotionally depleted that it is not possible to risk even the "Yes, I want to be well." The wonder that breaks upon us in this incident is that Jesus Christ is able to heal just such a person. His grace is good enough and strong enough to find the man by Bethesda pool. We have here a portrayal not so much of the search of faith, as we witnessed in the official from Capernaum, but rather of the search of grace. Jesus is able to find us where we are. He finds Nathanael, he finds the woman at the well, he finds this lonely man. Jesus heals him solely because of his own decision. The man does not even know Jesus' name.

Following the healing the event becomes very complicated. The day is the Sabbath and the man now made well is in trouble for breaking a law he probably never had worried about before. The good result of the healing—namely, his ability to walk and carry his mat—has now posed a new set of crises. Jesus once again finds the man. This time he identifies himself to the man and also unites his physical and spiritual self into a whole: "See you are well! Sin no more, that nothing worse befall you."

The interpretation of this sentence which contends that Jesus is saying that the man was thirty-eight years ill because he had sinned is countermanded by Jesus' own rejection of that thesis in John 9. What then does the sentence mean? I believe it should be seen in its larger theological sense: Jesus is saying that wholeness is not only a physical matter but that being well involves the whole self: moral, spiritual and physical.

We saw this same wholeness teaching in the encounter with the woman at the well. She is not permitted by Christ to accept the living water as a spiritual experience without the discovery of who she is as a person interrelated with the people in her life. Jesus drew together the moral, emotional, spiritual and relational parts of her life into a whole. Therefore she discovers the good news that living water is being offered to her real self—not to a phantom person or a "religious" person. We see now in this Bethesda incident the same wholeness teaching; Jesus first grapples with the man's physical crisis. That cure, because of the Sabbath day rules, plunges him into a religious and ethical crisis. But John tells us that Jesus finds the man again and tells him of the crisis graver than the paralysis of his legs and that is the bondage to sin.

The man immediately bears his own witness to Jesus by returning to the leaders of the Temple and telling the truth to them—that it was Jesus who had told him to break Sabbath traditions. The witness of the Samaritan woman (chapter 4) resulted in faith in Christ from the Samaritan city; this witness results in hostility, because Jesus had apparently broken the Sabbath observance tradition. John makes the point very clear: "this was why the Jews persecuted Jesus, because he did this on the Sabbath" (v. 16).

John's account faces the issue head on. Jesus has consciously challenged the observance of the traditions of the people concerning Sabbath Law and especially the Pharisee party to whom observance of the law was a non-negotiable keystone to their theology and life. Jesus Christ has found them where they are and the result is a deep uneasiness and hostility.

As we have observed up to this point throughout the Gospel, Jesus has been breaking through the barriers that surround people. In each of these instances there exists that tense moment at the edge of discovery from which we move either toward faith or toward hostility. There is no easy way to discover the meaning of life. It is at first humiliating for Nicodemus to realize that he must be born again; but as the first wonder of the promise dawns upon him, he realizes that he *may* be born again—that indeed the kingdom is for him and he is invited to enter it afresh. But the *edge* between Jesus' disappointing our old conclusions and convictions and the fulfillment of our deepest longings involves cost; the pathway that is open to all who would enter is hard to accept when it seems to lead in a direction apparently opposite to where we thought it should go. This is the dilemma in every encounter of people with Jesus Christ, whether it is the Pharisee, John the Baptist, or the man from Capernaum.

11. Four Witnesses
John 5:16–47

The temple leaders are hostile for two reasons: first, because Jesus broke the Sabbath and second, because he "also called God his Father, making himself equal with God." John records for us a long teaching discourse in which Jesus takes very seriously the theological objections made against his healing act on the Sabbath.

The fourth commandment of Moses' Law tells Israel, "Six days you shall labor, and do all your work; but the seventh day is a Sabbath to the Lord your God; in it you shall not do any work" (Deut. 5:13–14). "Sabbath" is a transliteration of a Hebrew word meaning "cease," so the command is clear; it is given by God in our favor because it is his will that there shall be a rhythm of life between work and rest.

This command had taken on very particular importance by the time of the first century and would remain throughout the first century a continual source of controversy among the leaders of Jewish thought. We have records of a meeting toward the end of the century of four distinguished rabbis, Gamaliel II, Joshua ben Chananiah, Eliezer ben Azariah, and Aquiba. They met in Rome to discuss the question—even then still a hotly debated one— whether or not God observes his own law, with special focus upon Sabbath Law. These rabbis agreed with traditional Jewish thought expressed by Philo of Alexandria, a first-century Jewish writer and a contemporary of New Testament writers, that God himself does not rest on the Sabbath. Philo writes: "For God never ceases creating, but as it is the property of fire to burn and of snow to be cold, so it is the property of God to create." He further explains that the divine "rest" of God does not mean that God abstains from doing good deeds or from his role as judge of all. (See C. H. Dodd for an extensive discussion of first-century Jewish thought on this matter, *The Interpretation of the Fourth Gospel*, pp. 320 ff.).

The question of what constitutes human work and therefore what becomes a violation of Sabbath Law was also a highly volatile issue in the first century. The Pharisee party had developed their own carefully catalogued list of Sabbath regulations, but we know from the Dead Sea Scrolls that the Essenes maintained rules that were even more stringent then the Pharisees. In the case of the man by the pool of Bethesda, he is in violation of Mishnaic tractate Sabbath 7:2, "the carrying of things from one domain to another," and also 10:5, "the carrying of an empty bed is forbidden" (Brown, *Gospel According to John*, p. 208).

Following the incident at Bethesda pool, John records for us the hostile reaction of some of those who were present. "This is why the Jews persecuted Jesus . . . because he not only broke the Sabbath . . . making himself equal with God" (vv. 16–18).

It becomes clear, that some of those who learned about Jesus' healing on the Sabbath are beginning to sense the larger implications of what others may have seen only as rebellion against Sabbath practices. John records this growing awareness of the larger issues involved, and it becomes vividly clear now as the speech of Jesus unfolds.

The first point that Jesus makes is his claim that what he does in his ministry is in full accordance with the will of God. On the basis of this premise, Jesus has given answer to their objections. He has placed Sabbath observance into its larger setting. God preserves his own prerogative to work his work on the Sabbath; when, therefore, this occurs, the Sabbath has not been broken. The larger truth at stake here is not the Sabbath but whether in fact Jesus Christ has the authority to be Lord of the Sabbath. Members of the group who hear him see immediately the force of his words.

In this discourse Jesus lays claim to this divine authority to work on the Sabbath and to judge. Note the main elements in his teaching:

(1) The Son does the will of God (v. 19).

(2) The Father loves the Son (v. 20).

(3) The Father gives authority to the Son (v. 21).

(4) The Son deserves honor from all the earth because it is God's will that humanity should honor and trust in the Son (v. 23).

(5) Life is given to those who believe in the Father and the Son (vv. 24–26).

(6) The Son is judge because in him is fulfilled the messianic prophecy (v. 27).

Following these claims, Jesus makes the statement that his

claims are not established simply because he has spoken them but because of "him who sent me." Then he describes how his ministry is validated to mankind as follows:

(1) First he reminds his listeners of the witness of John the Baptist (vv. 33–35). He describes John as a "burning and shining light." Jesus reminds them that temporarily John was popular and the people rejoiced in his light "for a while." The implication is that later, when John's message became harder and when John was himself arrested, his following diminished.

(2) Jesus then turns attention to the "works which the Father has granted me to accomplish" (v. 36). What Jesus does in his ministry of word and work bears witness to who he is.

(3) Jesus next points to the witness of the Father himself who "has borne witness to me." This is a reference to the divine witness to Jesus at his baptism and also forms the beginning of what later in the Gospel (chapter 14) will become clear as the confirming and authenticating ministry of the Holy Spirit.

(4) Jesus also mentions the Holy Scriptures (to Jesus' listeners the Old Testament). They validate Jesus Christ—"it is they that bear witness to me" (v. 39). He goes on to say that those who love the Law will see in Jesus the Law's true fulfillment.

This long speech by Jesus in John's Gospel, as well as other long discourses to be found later in the book, has posed a problem for many New Testament interpreters. There are some who are hesitant to accept them as speeches of Jesus Christ per se but see them rather as theological teaching of the Gospel writer placed into the book in the form of discourses. It is such a technique that Plato makes use of in *The Republic,* presenting his own philosophical teaching in the speeches of his beloved teacher Socrates. Critics who hold such a view point up the stylistic contrast between the Johannine discourses and the speeches of Jesus recorded in Matthew, Mark and Luke.

The difference in language style is not so important an argument, however, when we recognize that the Synoptic writers have tended to avoid all discourses in favor of an epigrammatic summary method of reporting. The classic example of this is found in Matthew 5, 6, and 7 (see also Luke 6). Matthew's record of the Sermon on the Mount omits discussion, give and take, and the gradual development of the ideas; instead what we have are the highpoints of Jesus' teaching tightly summarized with crisp epigrams. In contrast, what we see in John is the gradual emergence of themes through dialogue, debate, questions, event. Memorable epigrams are still present, but the speeches are more intimate, and use the kind of language expression we expect in interpersonal communication.

Could John have remembered these speeches and then have recorded them with reasonable accuracy? Leon Morris has discussed the first-century proficiency in memorization and verbal recall that has well documented the capacity of disciples to recall faithfully the teaching and dialogue of their teachers. Morris extensively discusses first-century Jewish teaching methods and quotes from the work of H. Riesenfeld, "The Gospel Traditions and Its Beginnings," in this regard. (Leon Morris, *The Gospel According to John*, p. 130 ff.). The strongest evidence we have in favor of the speeches as authentic records of the actual words of Jesus is that John presents them that way. His accuracy on small points, such as the porches at Bethesda, strengthens our confidence in his accuracy on the speeches of his teacher that are of far greater importance to him.

Jesus reaches the high point of his popular ministry as a result of this miracle of the feeding of the five thousand.

12. The King Everyone Wanted
John 6:1–15

A rather indefinite time description prepares us for the next event in the narrative. "Sometime later," John tells us (v.1, NEB), Jesus went across the Sea of Galilee. There is a time lapse between the events and discussion in chapter 5 and this incident recorded in chapter 6, and now the Passover is at hand. If the feast mentioned in chapter 5 was Pentecost or even Tabernacles, then we have a several-month lapse in the chronological sequence. Some interpreters take care of this gap by exchanging the order of chapters 5 and 6. This is the suggestion of Schnackenburg, Bultmann and others. Manuscript evidence, however, does not support this reordering; therefore we conclude that John has omitted several months in his narrative. He now brings us to the Sea of Galilee, which he also names the Sea of Tiberias—another example of his factual asides to aid Greek-Roman readers of his Gospel.

Where exactly does this incident of the feeding of the five thousand take place? Luke sets the place near Bethsaida (Luke 9:10–17) on the northern side of Galilee Lake, whereas John implies that the event occurs near Tiberias, a city on the southwest side of the lake (v. 23). At any rate, boats come from Tiberias to the site. In either case the event takes place in the countryside away from both cities, yet near the sea.

As we have noted in previous accounts, John shows interest in specific details, such as the reference to the ships coming over from Tiberias and the naming of particular disciples—Philip and Andrew and the part they take in the event. He also supplies us with the information that the barley loaves and fish came from a lad that Andrew had met. Each of these details is unique to John's account.

John insists that a miracle has occurred here—they "filled twelve baskets with fragments from the five barley loaves." This

68

event cannot be interpreted as an example of the impact of one lad's willingness to share inspiring the rest of the people to share as well. John here describes a sign by which Jesus himself—not because the people requested it, but because of his own decision— feeds the great crowd of people.

Jesus invites his disciples to share in the event, first by the question to Philip. Philip is immobilized by the hopelessness of the task. His estimate is two hundred days' work necessary to earn enough money to buy bread for such a crowd (one denarius per days' work was the traditional pay of a laborer in the first century). Andrew speaks up to tell the Lord about a boy who has five barley loaves and two fish, but then he catches himself and takes back even that suggestion. But Jesus makes use of Andrew's tentative offer, and it is that offer which becomes the raw material of this most impressive of all the public miracles of Jesus. Jesus does not create bread, he multiples a bread they already have. Barley is the bread of the poor. Wheat bread was more common. Jesus gives thanks (the Jews regularly gave thanks to God for their food) and then, as Luke records the incident, the food is distributed by the disciples to the people. John tells us that a surplus is left over.

There is no single event in the narratives of the New Testament that so completely welded the people's attention. Each Gospel records this incident and each recognizes the unique importance of the sign among the people, who say, "This is indeed the prophet who is to come into the world!" Once again we have the strong echo of the Malachi 4 messianic expectation of Israel. Jesus' act has convinced them of that kingly fulfillment, and the next sentence in John's account tells us that the people want forceably to make Jesus king.

At this point, let us reflect upon the nature of first-century messianic expectations. There are four threads that converge into the feelings and folk dreams of first-century Israel. Each of these four threads plays its role in John's narratives.

(1) The most primitive yearning is what might be described as the Abrahamic thread. This thread goes back to the very beginning of their history. In ancient Babylon Abram is chosen by God to become the founder of a new people. The Torah tells of his call, the promises made by God to him and his children (Gen. 12:1-3), his change of name. In Abraham the Jews have their identity sealed by the rite of circumcision which acknowledges the covenant God made to bless his people. In John 8:31-59 we have a stormy encounter of Jesus with the Pharisees about this great memory.

(2) Moses is both the deliverer of the people from bondage and

the law giver. The Mosaic thread is very deep in the character of first-century expectation. We see it represented in the yearly feasts, especially Passover and Pentecost, which celebrate the giving of the Law. The Pharisee movement has focused attention upon the importance of the covenant of law. In chapter 5:45–47 we observed that Jesus affirmed his own solidarity with this Mosaic thread— "for he wrote of me." In John 6:32 Jesus will again interpret the significance of Moses as the forerunner of himself. Again in chapter 7:16–24 Jesus dares to portray his own acts on the Sabbath as the true fulfillment of the meaning of the law and the fulfillment of the rite of circumcision.

(3) The third thread has to do with the memory of David and the kingdom. David the king gave to Israel its great moment of glory, and from that golden age the memory and hopes of the Jews stayed alive to the expectation that the glory could again be theirs. These deep-seated hopes are the foundation of first-century nationalism. They are also one source of negative attitudes toward outsiders. In the desire of the people to make Jesus king, we see them surfacing. The kingdom-yearning of the Pharisee Nicodemus is Davidic. This thread in the fabric of the people's feelings is easily stirred up, either to hope, as in the miracle of multiplication of loaves, or to fury, as when Jesus seemed to threaten the tribe's identity by his openness to Samaritans and foreigners. The feast of Hanukkah is in this sense a Davidic feast, in that it focuses upon nationalistic dreams of final victory.

(4) The fourth thread is the great prophetic tradition which, in a sense, synthesizes the other great threads: Abrahamic, Mosaic, Davidic. "This is indeed the *prophet . . .*" is a reference to the hope that one like Elijah would come and usher in the fulfillment of Abraham, Moses and David. *Messiah*, which is an Aramaic word meaning "anointed one" used only in John's Gospel, is a word that expresses this search for God's intervention in behalf of his people so that the great threads of their history might be fulfilled.

Verse 15 of chapter 6 might be called the high-water mark of Jesus' popularity with the people. The lines of the past have converged and intermingled with their present frustrations and hopes. Jesus has won them! Now begins in our Gospel a series of surprises. The first is abrupt and clear cut: Jesus declines their attempt to make him king. He simply absents himself from them—"Jesus withdrew again to the hills by himself."

The reader may be truly baffled by Jesus' response. We thought that his purpose was to win to himself a following, yet when the possibility of a mass people movement is a real opportunity, Jesus consciously and deliberately destroys the movement at its very origins. John offers no explanation. He simply states the fact that Jesus shunned the nationalistic fervor of this great crowd.

All that we are able to do as interpreters of the event is to note that mixed together in this account are two portrayals of the authority of Jesus Christ. His authority is shown by the miracle of the feeding of the five thousand and his authority is shown by his sovereign withdrawal. Jesus *will* help the people and he does so in the feeding of the five thousand. He *will not* become their king when they press this option upon him. Both of these are decisions by Jesus Christ the Lord.

Fyodor Dostoevsky has captured the profound implications of this decision by Jesus in the parable he puts in the mouth of Ivan in *The Brothers Karamazov*. Ivan the atheist, recently back from Paris, meets his devoutly Christian younger brother Alyosha, and seeks to prove to Alyosha how irrelevant is Jesus to the real events and forces of history. In the harsh dialogue of that noontime meeting Ivan tells his brother of a dream he had that proves the irrelevancy of Christ. This dream is in the form of a parable in which the devil once again meets Jesus. The devil is portrayed as the grand inquisitor of the Spanish inquisition. When Jesus comes to Spain, the inquisitor is unruffled by his appearance. He proceeds to interpret to Jesus where he failed. According to the inquisitor, the failure of Jesus occurs precisely at this point in John's Gospel—when Jesus refused to become king, when he refused to maintain that kingship by turning the rocks to bread. He points out to Christ that the people would never abandon such a king so long as he continued to give them bread. Because mankind wants and needs bread above every other thing. "You misunderstand man—you made him free when he wanted to be happy."

Dostoevsky has recognized a major theological ingredient in these two signs of authority by Jesus. The first sign shows the power of Christ and by it he wins the affection of the people. The second sign shows the freedom of Christ and by it he baffles the people. By this second sign Jesus has refused to possess our affection by power. The power that Jesus is able to make use of in our behalf is not like power as we know it. His power does not destroy our freedom. This is the theological result of the second sign of the authority of Jesus. Jesus does not need to be made our king—he already is.

13. A Storm
John 6:16–24

The disciples of Jesus were probably as confused by the events by the lake as was the great crowd. Up to this moment in his ministry haven't his signs all led inexorably toward just the kind of public response they have just witnessed? This would make the withdrawal of Jesus a keen disappointment. We feel a gradual and gathering momentum up to this point. Though there is a certain amount of opposition, there has been a steady growth of Jesus' popularity with the people at large. The fact that so large a crowd had gathered to hear and see Jesus is itself an example of his growing popularity.

John tells us that the disciples then embark across the sea toward Capernaum. This incident is also recorded for us with some differences in detail in Matthew 14:22–27 and Mark 6:45–51. Matthew and Mark both tell us that it is Jesus who commanded his disciples to take the boat. Mark says they were headed toward Bethsaida; however, both Mark and Matthew agree they finally landed at Gennesaret, which is just south of Capernaum. Matthew gives us the account of Peter who walks on the water to meet Jesus. John's account is the briefest, yet it nevertheless contains characteristic Johannine features such as his insistence that the boat arrived at Capernaum. In each account Jesus frightens the disciples in this middle-of-the-night meeting (3:00 A.M. by Mark's reckoning). But Jesus comforts them: "It is I; do not be afraid."

Why this event? It becomes a very personal sign and the first one in John's Gospel that is given only for the disciples. No one else is permitted to look on, which is not the case with the other signs of the authority and love of Christ. It is true that the people on the next day cannot understand how Jesus crossed the sea to Capernaum, but there are no answers given to their questions either by Jesus or his disciples.

Perhaps the disciples needed this intensely personal experience of their Lord in order to clear their heads after the confusing events of the previous day.

Up to this point, the disciples have been Jesus' followers. They each chose to follow Jesus and become his disciple. Much of the time they have been baffled by his message and his acts. John preserves this for us in his aside comment about their reactions in the woman at the well incident. Now at 3:00 A.M. they each receive at first the frightening but later the joyous confirmation of who Jesus is and of who they are. He has sought them out, at sea even! He has cared enough about them to find them and assure them of their own worth. In relational psychological terms, this event is a "stroke" for the disciples—a warm positive assurance of their belovedness to Jesus. There is the mixture in the incident of *fear, surprise and joy*. These emotions very often coincide. But when the shock of recognition is resolved, "they were glad to take him into the boat."

This incident is an interlude that shows to us the warmth and sensitivity of Jesus. It also gives to us a traumatic and intensely personal experience of Jesus as the "I am"—"It is I"—*ego eimi*.

14. The Hard Words

John 6:25–71

Back across the lake at Capernaum, the crowd finds Jesus, and they call him *Lord*: "Lord, give us this bread always" (v. 34). Many have followed him from across the lake; such a show of faith we have rarely witnessed in the Gospel. But there is a menacing insistence in their affection that is demanding and threatening. They call Jesus Lord, yet they insist upon a certain sign which for them has become all important. They have been won to the bread-giver Lord, and that is the Lord they desire. In other words, these people have formed a clear image in their minds of the form that Messiah will take, and for the present moment Jesus of Nazareth is the one who adequately fulfills that expectation. But the implication is clear—once Jesus no longer satisfies their expectations, then their praise will turn to wrath.

They have a faith that is responding to what they are looking for, but it is not a faith that is willing to be taught and molded by the Lord they seek. This one-sidedness of their faith becomes clear as the dialogue continues and as Jesus refuses to accomodate himself to their dreams.

This narrative shows us theologically that Jesus Christ as the object of our faith is not only the one who fulfills our deepest hopes—he also surprises them and asserts his authority over them. These people who honor him as the giver of bread will not be willing to hear his next teaching. Jesus will become irrelevant to them just as soon as his words veer away from their request, so that by the close of this very chapter John tells us that most of them will have gone home disillusioned and bitter.

Jesus accuses these temporary followers of having not really understood the *sign*, but rather of having been charmed and intrigued by the miracle—"not because you saw signs, but because you ate your fill of the loaves" (v. 26). They did not see the meaning that was at the core of the event.

What is it that is so disappointing to them? The disappointment sets in when Jesus makes one great fact really clear: that he is not the bread-giver, he is the bread itself! This is the turning point, and it still is. Jesus Christ is not the answer to our great questions, because in that case *we* are the ones who raise all of the questions, and in so doing we begin the process of drawing Jesus into the manipulative circle of our control. He is the Lord, and that is a far larger matter.

There are multitudes who will welcome Jesus as the answer, as the teacher, as the friend, as the bread-giver, but when it comes to the embarrassing central question—who is he really?—they draw back. Is Jesus Christ really essential to us once we have the benefits he confers? The Gospel of John has brought the issue sharply to center stage by this record of the words of Jesus. Jesus will not belong even to the expectations of the devout. We are to belong to him. He will not be the teacher whose words we are to treasure, or whose powerful gifts we are to enjoy. He is instead the very Lord of life without whom there is no life. Jesus is not the cake of life—a luxury for those who have time and money to dabble in religion. Jesus is the barley bread; the poor people's bread; the basic and totally essential source of life itself. We cannot survive without him.

And yet this Lord invites his disciples to become identified with him fully, completely, intimately.

That is how we interpret the parts of this dialogue where Jesus speaks of the disciples eating his flesh. These are hard words, in that they cannot be easily classified into existing categories by his listeners; only if they are willing to trust his character will they manage to stay with him after such opaque teaching. The context of the passage gives good reason to conclude that Jesus' intention was to create just such a credibility crisis for those who surrounded him, so that they might realize the radical nature of his claims. The reason we conclude this is that Jesus closes his dialogue with the haunting question to his disciples, "Will you also go away?" It is Peter who answers: "Lord, to whom shall we go?" Here is a sentence that does not demand of Jesus certain or special signs. Rather it is a sentence of simple faith. There is not an ounce of triumphalism in it, only the confidence of one disciple that Jesus Christ himself is Lord, therefore Peter will trust him.

New Testament scholarship has observed the possible relationship between this discourse and early church sacramental teaching. Raymond Brown (*Gospel According to John*, pp. 291 ff.) and C. H. Dodd (*The Interpretation of the Fourth Gospel*) both have surveyed the history of New Testament interpretation on this connection. (See also Calvin, *Commentary . . . on John*, pp. 267 ff.).

15. Problematic Jews
John 7:1–36

After his great miracle of feeding, the brothers of Jesus urge him to go to Jerusalem in order to prove his messiahship—"that your disciples may see the works you are doing . . . show yourself to the world" (vv. 3–4). The point is that Jesus has done his great sign only in the region of Galilee. John's comment upon their suggestion is as brief as it is sharp: "For even his brothers did not believe in him." They do not trust the strategy of Jesus which keeps him primarily in the region of Galilee whereas the really important decision makers are at Jerusalem.

We were told in Luke at the close of Jesus' temptation by the devil, that "when the devil had ended every temptation, he departed from him until an opportune time" (Luke 4:13).

Here at the high point of Jesus' fame in Galilee we recall the earlier temptations of Jesus by Satan and see echoes of them, somewhat disguised, though equally forceful and dangerous as they had been in the deserts near Jordan.

(1) Jesus was hailed as king (John 5:15) and the crowds wanted to present to him a kingship of their making. But Jesus rejects their offer of kingdom as he had rejected Satan's offer (Luke 4:6–8). He will be king on his own ground.

(2) Jesus is urged by the crowds to give them bread: "Lord, give us this bread always" (John 6:34). He does not grant the bread they desired, though he offers to them the opportunity for the Eternal bread. Jesus had answered Satan's challenge in a very similar way. To Satan he quoted Deuteronomy 8:3 which held out even to Satan the greater bread that comes from God.

(3) Now in chapter 7 Jesus is tempted by his own brothers to prove his kingly authority in Jerusalem. They develop a logic in their challenge to Jesus that sounds very much as if it were quoted from Jesus' own words recorded in the Book of Matthew: "No one

lights a lamp and places it under a basket." Jesus' brothers tell him, "For no man works in secret if he seeks to be known openly." Jesus does not accept their counsel, just as he did not accept the devil's most dangerous temptation when he urged Jesus to win the people by a great leap from the roof of the temple. That temptation in Galilee is more subtle, in that it is a proposal that appeals to the good purpose of Jesus to win the people to the truth. How could a better means be found than for the people to see the Psalm 91 prophecy fulfilled at temple square?

> For he will give his angels charge of you
> to guard you in all your ways.
> On their hands they will bear you up,
> lest you dash your foot against a stone.
>
> (Psalm 91:11, 12)

Jesus has won against these hard temptations. They are all the more dangerous because they come from the adoring crowds and from his own brothers. We know from the Book of Acts (Acts 1:14) that these brothers of Jesus will later trust him and that they become disciples too, but at this point they do not trust him. They do not trust Jesus to set his own pace and to live out his kingly reign as he decides. They are like the crowds in chapter 6 who have tasted power and it is power that they want to see.

This will not be the last time that Jesus must face temptation. It is also true that his disciples will face temptations, as the Book of Acts will make clear. The temptation to power, we know from our own Christian experience, has continued through history to our present age as well.

John has now drawn a distinction for us between the faith of the official from Capernaum and the "faith" of the crowd and the brothers of Jesus. The man from Capernaum persists in faith to hold on to hope, to bring his need to Christ, and to claim the love of Christ. When Jesus does not go down to the official's city, as he had earnestly requested—"come down before my child dies"— nevertheless he trusts in Jesus. But the "faith" of the crowds and of the brothers of Jesus after the feeding demands the sign they have in mind and does not trust Jesus when he seems to contradict the demand. This second form of persistence in John's Gospel is seen as unbelief. Faith brings our whole self to Jesus Christ, asking for help, and then trusts in the love of Christ. But our demand for certain signs as tests of the validity of his love is not faith according to John. Jesus speaks the same words he had used in Cana at the wedding party—"My time has not yet come." This may also be translated "It is not yet time for me." This phrase has special significance in John's account, and now, because of its repetitious use by Jesus and John, we begin to realize its larger purpose within the Gospel.

Though Jesus tells his brothers that he will not go up to the Feast of Tabernacles (a feast held at the end of September and beginning of October commemorating the wilderness wanderings), nevertheless after they have gone to Jerusalem he does go secretly, toward the middle of the eight-day feast.

But in Jerusalem Jesus teaches openly at the temple during the feast. His sermon has two great parts as recorded in chapter 7. Part one of the discourse is spoken at the middle of the feast. It answers questions about the source of Jesus' authority with particular focus upon his apparent breaking of the Sabbath. He makes a connection between the traditional rite of circumcision which may be performed on the Sabbath (and so is "work" done on the Sabbath) and his healing. Why, Jesus reasons, has he been accused of breaking the law, when a man's whole body has been made well (the man at the pool of Bethesda)? The point Jesus makes is that just as the rite of circumcision was done in order not to violate the law of Moses, so also his act of grace was done in order not to violate the law of Moses. Jesus tells his listeners that he has fulfilled the kindly intent and purpose of the law of Moses on that Sabbath just as the priests have in performing the ceremony of circumcision on the Sabbath. The teaching of Jesus produces a mixed reaction.

In this scene we meet for the first time in the Gospel members of the Sadducee party (the high priest's group; see comments on 3: 1–21). During the period of the Syrian occupation of Judea, the priestly faction had made great compromises. One of the reasons the lay movement (the Pharisees) had originally emerged came from the attempt of deeply concerned people to hold on to the true worship of Yahweh at a time when even the priests of the temple had abandoned the heritage of Israel. Later, during the time of Maccabean reign, the priests were able once again to reestablish their primacy in the temple. The irony in this incident is that we notice here the beginning signs of a coalition of fear that will begin to form between the crafty Sadducees and the earnest though rigid and self-righteous Pharisees.

At the Feast of Tabernacles Jesus
makes a great promise that baffles
his listeners.

16. The Living Water
John 7:37–52

On the last day of the feast, Jesus preaches a second sermon. The sermon is one of the briefest of the discourses of Jesus as they appear in John's Gospel.

"If any one thirst, let him come to me and drink." Let us think for a moment about some of the dynamics present in that very first sentence. Earlier in this chapter we saw that Jesus preserves his own freedom. We might call that the freedom of God. The crowds and even his own family cannot control his ministry. "The light shines in the darkness, and the darkness has not overcome it" (1:5). His *own* decisions determine his goals, not our faith or our unbelief.

C. S. Lewis has captured this freedom of Christ in his remarkable Chronicles of Narnia. The creator and ruler of Narnia is Aslan, the Great Lion, "son of the Emperor from beyond the sea." Though these stories may—and should—be read first of all as exciting adventures, Lewis's theological perspectives become clear in the experiences of the Narnians and of the English children who visit Narnia.

In *The Silver Chair* (pp. 16–17), when Jill first meets Aslan she is terrified. This great lion sits like one of the lions of Trafalgar Square beside a stream of cold water. She is desperately thirsty, yet the lion is so close to the stream that taking a drink is an impossible option for her. She is even more shocked when the great lion speaks to her: "You may drink if you are thirsty." Jill wants to drink but her fear makes her hold back. She asks if the lion will promise not to do anything while she drinks. Aslan answers her, "I make no promise."

In this answer may be seen something of the profound theological content we have discovered in John's Gospel. The Great Lion holds out the kingly offer of water to Jill, yet he preserves his own freedom. Jill must trust Aslan—and she finally does.

The disciples of Jesus make the same discovery. Jesus will not necessarily become the king we want. He will not promise to keep a safe distance from the stream. That is because he is the stream. Jill cannot know that great prior fact at the beginning of her encounter with Aslan. Neither do the great crowds at Galilee understand who this Jesus really is. They receive a difficult yet profoundly important sign of his kingship when he will not be their king on their terms. They have met up with his kingly freedom. Jesus Christ possesses a freedom from and beyond their expectations.

But as John in his Gospel makes the freedom of Christ a major theme, so at the same time he is equally insistent upon a second, concurrent theme—that is, the freedom of discipleship. Jesus calls disciples to follow him, but they make their own decisions of belief or unbelief. The freedom thread in discipleship is preserved throughout the Gospel.

C. S. Lewis has understood this concurrent nature of the two freedoms in his stories of Narnia. Aslan never cancels out Jill's choice about the stream. "You may drink if you are thirsty," he tells her. In *The Horse and His Boy* (p. 157), the lad Shasta, who has sensed a large presence walking along side of him on a steep mountain pass in the middle of a dense night fog, finally whispers out, "Who are you?" The great golden voice of Aslan answers, "One who has waited long for you to speak." Our rightful authority is not destroyed by the authority of Jesus Christ.

The sermon of Jesus on the seventh day of the feast of Tabernacles begins with the two freedoms bound together. "If anyone thirst . . . " In other words, if we have ears to hear, then the word is spoken to us. If we are thirsty, we may come. The Sermon on the Mount contains the same offer: "Blessed are those who hunger and thirst . . . " (Matt. 5:6/Luke 6:21). The offer is universal and the only requirement is our decisive choice. Those who may come are those who choose to come because they are thirsty. Both the awareness of thirst and the choice to drink are therefore important signs of freedom.

Jesus has invited his temple listeners to come to him and to drink. This evangelistic sentence is followed by a quotation: "He who believes in me, as the scripture has said, 'Out of his heart shall flow rivers of living water.' " What text in the scriptures is Jesus now quoting? There is no Septuagint or Hebrew passage in the Old Testament that reads precisely in the words of this sentence. In fact, one of the problems we have in fixing this quotation with certainty is that there are so many different Old Testament references to the promise of water. The prophets Ezekiel (47:1–11) and

Zechariah (14:11) both speak of the gift of water in messianic terms. Jesus' quotation recalls a large body of Old Testament expectation concerning water as the sign of the Lord's coming.

Perhaps our best clue to the intent of Jesus' quotation is to appreciate the practices that take place during the traditional observances of the Feast of Tabernacles in first-century Jerusalem. Jesus has taken hold of the present celebration of the people in order to fulfill the hidden prophetic meaning in their celebration. The significance of water is highlighted ceremonially during this feast, as the Jews recall God's provision of water from the rock in the desert wanderings (Num. 20:2–13). Each morning the procession of pilgrims sings one of the Hallel psalms (Psalm 114) which recalls how God granted water to his people during the exodus.

For the seven days of the feast, water is carried in a golden pitcher from the pool of Siloam to the temple, as a reminder of God's provision of water to his people in the wilderness. Perhaps it is at that ceremonial moment that Jesus Christ announces to the people that he is the one who is the fulfillment of what that ceremony celebrates. We can empathize with the yearning for water in an arid land as the sign of God's redemption. In the Dead Sea scrolls we see the messianic yearnings of the Qumran community also expressed in terms of water: "I thank thee, O Lord, because thou has put me at a source of flowing streams in dry ground" (quoted in Morris, *Gospel According to John*, p. 411).

There is a grammatical problem in this sermon. Is Jesus teaching that out of Jesus Christ himself will come the living water? Or, is he teaching that as the disciples have faith, then out of their life will flow living water? Raymond Brown (*Gospel According to John*, pp. 320–21) points up the various translation possibilities for this sentence. He chooses a translation option which keeps the text open to both possibilities.

John follows his quotation of the Lord's sermon with his own comment which preserves theologically the total sense of the passage. John tells us that his "living water" in the disciples is in fact the real presence of Christ within their lives, and he introduces a preliminary statement about the Holy Spirit as the one who will be given to the believers when Christ has been glorified. Later in this Gospel the Lord himself will speak in a detailed way about the person and work of the Holy Spirit. John here introduces that whole subject but does not pursue it with his readers.

The result of this brief sermon is still more verbal conflict between the people about Jesus. We are indebted to John for his careful attention to the arguments that are raised against Jesus.

The Synoptic Gospels do not give to us as clear a picture of what were the points of actual strain and conflict between Jesus and some of his listeners. In these sentences following Jesus' sermon we note a few of those arguments:

(1) Is Christ to come from Galilee? Should he not come from Judea (v. 41)? This objection is based upon a lack of information concerning Jesus' tie to the city of David.

(2) Are you led astray too (v. 47)? There is a feeling among Pharisees, John tells us, that Jesus is leading people away from the true foundations of the Law and the true prophetic expectations.

There are also in the storm of controversy the signs of growing faith among certain of the listeners. This tension has made it impossible, evidently, to arrest Jesus.

Nicodemus appears a second time in the Gospel in this setting. He calls for justice and even-handedness among his colleagues, the Pharisees, but they reply to his statement with a snide "Are you from Galilee too?"

I am impressed by the fact that a result of growing faith in Nicodemus' life is a sensitivity to justice and fairness.

17. The Kingly Silence
John 7:53–8:11

We now consider a passage that has posed technical problems for all interpreters of the Gospel of John. This text does not appear in the principal Eastern manuscripts of the book. Nor is it found in the ancient Coptic manuscripts. But it is found in Western manuscripts: Jerome included it in the Latin Vulgate, and it appears in Codex Bezae (fifth century). Some manuscripts place this text in Luke's Gospel following 21:38, and some include the account at other places in John.

Some scholars argue that the language use is not Johannine, e.g., the phrase "scribes and Pharisees" is a typical Synoptic phrase but is not typical of John. The argument from language use is not at all conclusive, however, because there are features in the narrative that are very much at home in John's Gospel. The attention to detail is typical of John's narrative style. The literary practice of aside remarks made to the reader is typical—"they were posing this question to trap him." Moreover, the narrative is thematically plausible, and it fits into the sequence as an understandable event within the Feast of Tabernacles encounters.

Some critics have suggested that one reason this text may have been shunned by some of the scribal copiers of the early church was its theme. "It is plain enough that this passage was unknown anciently to the Greek churches . . . but as it is found in many old Greek manuscripts, and contains nothing unworthy of an Apostolic Spirit, there is no reason why we should refuse to apply it to our advantage" (Calvin, *Commentary on . . . John*, p. 319; see also Brown, *Gospel According to John*, p. 335). The text has stayed.

Let me argue for its inclusion right here at this place in the Gospel. I find helpful the hypothesis that this incident may have been suppressed because its content may have frightened certain of the early Christians as perhaps potentially dangerous and possible of misinterpretation. If this is so, it is a remarkable witness to the integrity of early church scribes that they faithfully recorded the ancient manuscripts with so few examples of such tampering with the original text. By the grace of God, there were enough ancient copiers who would not withdraw this text and who insisted upon keeping it in the Gospel. I do not feel there is justification in removing the text from John or placing it at any other position in the New Testament (i.e., in Luke). It has wide enough support in manuscript evidence.

We have noted the first two of Jesus' discourses in the temple. He is prepared to speak the third sermon when the scene is interrupted. John tells us that scribes and Pharisees bring to Jesus a woman caught in the act of adultery. This is our first mention in John's Gospel of "scribes." Some ancient manuscripts read here "chief priests" in the place of "scribes,"which seems more characteristic of John's writing style. From the evidence of chapter 7 we expect that members from the high priesthood, namely Sadducees, have joined in this challenge to Jesus. The term "scribes" is not descriptive of a party, and naturally all Pharisees are scribes, although it is possible there are scribes who may be independent of the Pharisee party.

A woman is brought to Jesus and a committee of leaders asks for his judgment on the case. They remind Jesus that in the Law the punishment for adultery is stoning (Lev. 20:10; Deut. 22:21; Ezek. 16:38–40). "What do you say about her?"

If the Law is clear then why is this case brought to Jesus? Teachers of the Law (rabbis) in the first century were consulted over obscure questions, not on such open-and-shut cases. This is why the fine points of Sabbath observances had so taken up the time of first-century lawyers. It was the obscurity of possible Sabbath violation that needed clarification. But in this instance, as the text makes clear, the woman was caught in the very crime. Therefore, presumably, the Law is clear. Why then this question to the teacher, interrupting Jesus' discourses?

John's aside comment shows that in his judgment the reason is clear enough. The Pharisees and the representation of the high priestly party have brought this human being to Jesus to interrupt him and to test him so that they will have grounds to accuse him. In chapter 6 we read that Jesus *tested* (same Greek word) Philip with his question—where will we find food? But the testing by Jesus is in order to establish Philip's faith upon solid ground, by stretching Philip's own resources to their limits. Now the word is used in the sense of to trap or to tempt, so that by the answer he makes Jesus will have destroyed himself.

What is the nature of this complicated testing? There are several dangerous possibilities for Jesus, each of which would prove destructive to him.

(1) The first possibility is the real danger that faces Jesus were he simply to agree to their literal reading of the Law. We have historical evidence that at about A.D. 30 the Romans denied to the Jewish religious courts the right of capital punishment. (John later refers to this ban in John 18:31.) Therefore, if Jesus were to authorize capital punishment, he would be guilty of breaking the Pax Romana—the order by which Rome was able to hold its vast Mediterranean Empire together against the chaos of anarchy.

(2) If Jesus were to disagree with the Law of Moses, how would he sustain his claim to truth? He has already walked a precarious edge on the question of Sabbath observance, but in that case the technical nature of the tradition worked to his favor. Now there are no major technical questions. A further point that intensifies the pressure of this test is the expectation of the people. They long for the prophet like Elijah. Remember it was Elijah who would allow no compromise with evil. He ordered death for the four hundred false prophets following his vindication in the great test against Baal (1 Kings 18:40). John the Baptist became popular with the people because he bravely challenged evil and called a spade a spade.

It can be shown with countless ancient and contemporary examples that a hard line against proven criminals is more popular with the people than a soft line. If it is Jesus' intent to win the people to himself, he now has the opportunity. He can prove his prophetic bravery by openly challenging Roman restraints. This will win for him the friendship of all Zealots and revolutionaries. He can show prophetic obedience to the Law by insisting upon its full measure of execution without compromise or equivocation. This will win the lawyers. He can win the people by providing for them a validated guilty person upon whom they may express the pent-up frustration, anger and guilt that they feel within their own hearts. This is his moment to become Elijah once and for all. But to go against the Law and set its justice aside in favor of this one woman will win few friends for Jesus.

(3) One further observation that we must make is a subtle but important point. The text shows us what the opposition to Jesus thinks of him and his teaching. They suspect that he will fall into

their trap, not because he will agree to their suggestion and urge the death of the sinner, but because he will favor a more kindly solution and thereby will stumble badly with both the Law and the people. In this sense, they are making use of the Law as it suits their purpose.

John tells us that this use of the Law is cynical, and for the purpose of tempting Jesus. Justice is not the concern of the crowd, because they have only brought the woman—where is the man? They are using this scandal of a noble relationship, not in order to honor the Law and marriage but to entrap Jesus Christ. We understand this method in our experiences when people, we or others, make use of a worthwhile issue or truth in order to entrap another person because we think that issue will most perfectly expose their vulnerability. Then it is that the Law is used not for its own worth or truth but in the same way as the Devil used Psalm 91—in order to tempt and to destroy the truth.

What is Jesus to do with this most vicious of the temptations he has faced? The narrative of John is eloquent by its spare use of words: Jesus "bent down and wrote with his finger on the ground." What is most dramatic about this moment is not what Jesus might have written on the ground—John does not give us any clues—but the fact that he is *silent*. This kingly silence, nerve-wracking and awesome, is the first sign we have in this account of the authority of Jesus Christ. He will not answer them, though he does not walk away to leave them to their own intentions; he stays his ground. His might and authority slows everything down. By this silence Jesus has focused the many possible motivations and ingredients of this angry scene upon himself. The agonizing silence shifts the attention of the crowd away from the woman to Jesus.

The crowd can endure the silence no longer. They press him to answer their question. "He stood up and said to them, 'Let him who is without sin among you be the first to throw a stone at her.'" Following this simple sentence, Jesus again writes on the ground. By his words he shifts the focus away from the woman and her guilt, away from himself, to the crowd that stands around her. He confronts the questioners with themselves and their own inner thirsts: we hear echoes of his words the day before: "Is anyone thirsty ... ?" Beginning with the oldest, John tells us, the crowd walked away.

One of the marks of youth is its sense of infallibility. Usually the older person recognizes his or her fraility and humanity more quickly than the young. One very substantial benefit of age is its mellowing effect. Jesus has performed a sign in behalf of the woman and in behalf of the crowd. The crowd has been temporarily humbled, their wrath restrained by the sovereign grace of Jesus Christ, their focus radically altered. The woman has been spared from the cynical punishment that the crowd had wanted. But there is more to this incident.

Jesus now speaks to the woman who has been left alone with him. He invites her to answer him. The Lord does not mock the Law or its profound concerns for the meaning of human relationships. "Woman, where are they? Has no one condemned you?" Jesus sets her free from condemnation and calls her to the way of righteousness. "Neither do I. . . . Go, and do not sin again." The scene is closed.

What has happened here is that one human being has gained ground while another has lost ground. As this woman has been set free from the mob and its violence, as she has experienced the forgiveness of Jesus Christ, she has gained a new and very deep freedom. But Jesus must pay the price for this grace. The crowd has been humiliated by the miracle of the shock of self-recognition, and Jesus will pay. He has identified himself with sinners.

One greater than Elijah is here. This new Elijah takes the place of the four hundred prophets. Just as their heavy punishment is due to fall upon them, he steps to their side and takes their place. This scene has prepared the path for the way of the cross.

*Jesus teaches about the true fulfill-
ment of the ancient Old Testament
yearning for light.*

18. The Light of the World
John 8:12-30

The brutal interruption is over. Jesus still stands in the courtyard of the Temple. Now he speaks to the people: "I am the light
of the world; he who follows me will not walk in darkness, but will
have the light of life."

The Feast of Tabernacles makes use of the symbolism of water,
as we have noted. But it also uses the symbol of light to recall the
great pillar of fire that had faithfully led the children of Israel during the wanderings in the wilderness. Each evening four great
lamps are lighted in the court of the women. (The Mishnah, Suk-
kah 5:2-4, tells of this ceremony, as does Josephus.) John tells us
in verse 20 that these teachings take place "in the temple precincts, in the treasury." This area is directly adjacent to the court
of the women in which the great lamps shine. The passage in
Zechariah 14, where we heard of the prophecy in connection with
the claim of Jesus to be the living water, also contains these words:
"And there shall be continuous day . . . for there shall be light even
in the evening" (v.7).

This passage shows clearly that in John's Gospel the image of
light is not the result of Gnostic or Stoic influence but comes out of
Old Testament prophetic imagery. Jesus uses the life experiences
of the people—in this case one of the joyous celebrations of their
year—and from these experiences draws together the images
which become elements in his teaching. He does this same kind of
teaching in the parables which draw upon common everyday life
experiences.

There is a deeper theological fact at work here, and that is the
fulfillment of what these great ceremonies symbolize. Four great
lamps that light up the night sky in Jerusalem are in themselves
spectacular, but the lamps are symbolic. Jesus Christ is the light of
the world, not in a symbolic sense but in reality.

Light, in the Exodus sense, is the pillar by which the people find their way. This is the very practical way in which the Jews thought of light and truth. Truth rightly leads the pilgrim not toward false paths but according to the will of God. Truth is not, therefore, simply a correct answer to a philosophical question; it is a word of wholeness—it has to do with intent, meaning, ultimate goal, the very will of God. This is why Jesus is correct and truthful in the whole biblical sense in his response to this situation forced upon him by the Pharisees and high priests. The purpose of God's Law is to lead God's people to the pathway of God's will. Jesus, therefore, will not answer the apparently simple question of the crowd: "What do you say about her?" because the question is not rooted in the desire to do God's will. In the Greek world, answering questions in an ideological sense is the way to truth—as in the dialogues of Plato—whereas the Hebrew sees the quest for truth in a total sense of will, action and thought.

John faithfully records for his readers the fact that Jesus' claim does not win over those who are against Jesus. Notice how the list of objections to Jesus continues to grow:

(1) You are bearing witness to yourself, therefore your witness cannot be true (v. 13). This is a fundamental objection to the *ego eimi* affirmations of Jesus. This objection is taken very seriously by Jesus in his self-disclosure teachings of 5:25–47, and in chapter 14.

(2) Where is your Father (v. 19)? Who are you (v. 25)? These last questions indicate a deeper kind of quest that is underway among many of those who were present at the temple discourses.

Themes that were present in the earlier two parts of the Feast discourse are repeated again. Jesus portrays his relationship with the Father in intimate and relationship terms: "He who sent me is with me; he has not left me alone, for I always do what is pleasing to him" (v. 29).

19. *Way of Freedom*
John 8:31–59

Although some who listened to Jesus' Feast of Tabernacles discourse rejected him (v.30), some respond positively. For them, Jesus returns to the idea of truth: "If you continue in my word, you are truly my disciples, and you will know the truth and the truth will make you free" (vv. 31–32).

Truth is meant here primarily in the Hebrew sense of "walking in the way of righteousness" rather than in the more intellectual Greek sense of "know the meaning of." Though this Hebrew underpinning is basic to our Lord's words, nevertheless his promise has profound implications for the more sophisticated concept of perception of truths. Jesus is saying to the Greek world that truth, as the reason or meaning behind and within all reality, is found as men and women obey God and God's speech. We are to continue, that is abide, in the word of Christ to us. It is this relationship that makes us disciples, and within that obedience we discover both the truth and its gift to us, freedom.

Jesus here teaches that to follow his way as a disciple means freedom for the disciple. Freedom is inseparable from truth. There cannot be freedom without righteousness. The woman caught in adultery experiences freedom from possible death because of the fact that Christ's righteousness, his truth, has made possible her freedom. Freedom is not seen as an automatic *given*, as a "general truth" (Dietrich Bonhoeffer, *The Cost of Discipleship*, p. 45), but rather as a result of discipleship. Jesus Christ himself grants freedom.

These words are not welcomed by the people. His listeners have caught the inference that until they enter the way of discipleship they are not truly free. Now we have the odd situation where the promise has hurt their feelings. They remember the ancient promises of blessing made by God to Abraham; therefore standing upon their tribal pride they disclaim any possibility that in this latter age they might need to be set free. "We are descendants of Abraham, and have never been in bondage to anyone. How is it that you say, 'You will be made free'?" These words are braver than they are realistic, but their point is clear. They are not encouraged by Jesus' promise. Jesus has stirred their disappointment by his suggestion that they still have need for truth and for freedom.

Jesus answers their disappointment not in nationalistic slogans but in simple personal terms: "every one who commits sin is a slave to sin." Jesus has cut through all of the advantages of an Abrahamic legacy. Tribal membership does not guarantee freedom. The advantages of tribe and heritage are thrown away by our sins which plunge us into the grasp of the bitter kingdom of slavery to evil. These are hard words for a tribal person to hear, because at the heart of tribalism is the conviction that there are special privileges that accompany special relationship. Jesus has informed his listeners that such a confidence is unfounded. When we sin—*whoever we are*—we are under sin's grasp, whether we are rich or poor, in the tribe or out of it. The nationalistic argument is simply irrelevant as far as Jesus is concerned.

One of the harshest arguments we have recorded between Jesus and the people results from this whole-scale challenge by Jesus to a very highly prized value in Jewish life. Jesus will startle his listeners with the statement that as they do the devil's will he is their father, since he is the author of untruth. This extreme sentence by Jesus should be understood in a hyperbolic sense, as we understand the charge against Peter by Jesus recorded in Matthew 16:23 —"But Jesus turned and said to Peter, 'Get behind me, Satan! You are a hindrance to me' "—because later in the dialogue, Jesus will assure them that he knows that Abraham is indeed their father (v. 56).

Jesus charges that the devil "was a murderer from the beginning, and has nothing to do with the truth, because there is no truth in him." I feel this sentence relates to the incident of the woman caught in adultery. By this connection, we rightly understand that earlier incident as a temptation of Jesus, motivated not simply by angry men who want blood but by the author of such murder—the devil himself. Jesus reminds his listeners that Satan has no interest in truth, though he asks many questions about truth. The dialogue finally centers on the relationship between Jesus and Abraham. Will Jesus cast out all meaning in the Abrahamic heritage which runs so deep in the memory and aspiration of the people?

One of the most dramatic of the great "I am" sentences of Jesus comes at the close of this dialogue. If we are willing to accept the shattering truth of Jesus' words, then we see Jesus Christ as the true author of Abraham's very identity and promise. Far from destroying the hopes and promises of Israel, it is Jesus himself who made the promises upon which Abraham trusted his life and heritage. "Jesus said to them, 'Amen, amen, I say to you, before Abraham was, I am' " (v. 58). Here Jesus speaks the great identity verb of Israel of and by itself—*Yahweh*.

*A man blind from birth is healed; in
the aftermath the question arises as
to who is truly blind.*

20. A Question of Blindness
John 9:1–41

While Jesus is still in Jerusalem, having concluded the Feast of Tabernacles discourse, he is walking with his disciples when he comes upon a man blind from birth, a young man (vv. 19–22). In this incident, as in the case of the man at the pool of Bethesda, Jesus takes the initiative to heal. The text tells us that it is Jesus who first notices the young man, though it is the disciples who first speak: "Rabbi, who sinned, this man or his parents, that he was born blind?"

The Book of Job should have settled this question for Israel, but still in the first century the popular folk-theology of the Jews saw a direct causal connection between illness and sins. The question of the disciples should be seen in the context of this connection, and they are asking of their rabbi his answer to that question. They will feel better if they have the fine point resolved in their minds.

There is also a second possibility. Their question may simply be the kind of conversation people make when they are embarrassed and feel helpless before a crisis. Perhaps Jesus has posed just this crisis for his disciples as he first finds the young man and stands silently for a few moments before him. The disciples feel the need to say something. Like people at the site of an automobile accident, the discussion of the accident is a form of release from the frustration of helplessness. Blindness is apparently so final and tragic. There is no real value in the discussion except to satisfy the technical curiosity of the disciples.

Jesus cuts short the dialogue with an immediate reply to their question. There are two parts to Jesus' answer. First, he rejects the line of reasoning that the disciples were pursuing concerning the young man's blindness. "It was not that this man sinned, or his parents." By this sentence Jesus has opened the way for a different understanding and outlook toward the tragedy of disability. In this

93

concrete instance, Jesus has separated illness from its causal relationship to sin, and thus prepares the way for a nondefeatist view of human illness. If my parents' sin is the cause, then how can I ever find help from what is seen as a just punishment? But if the illness stands by itself, then I am set free to challenge its grip.

It is obvious that there are illnesses that are the consequence of sinfulness. A drunken driver may, by his or her act, cause grave harm for a passenger in the car. In this case, the broken rib, leg and punctured spleen are caused by the parents' sin, if that passenger is their child. However, to concentrate upon correctly fixing the *source* of the crisis may be important in the courtroom but it has very little value in the emergency operating room. Don't waste the doctor's time with the sordid details of a late-night drinking spree and a wild car race done for the thrill of it! Jesus, the great physician that he is, separates the single human crisis he now faces from the scribal fascination with fixing blame.

The second part of Jesus' answer is the statement that even this crisis of blindness, as it is overcome by the authority of Christ, will work to the glory of God. Jesus does not say that blindness is good, but he does say that as it is now conquered by his word, he will show yet another sign of the will and purpose of God to work in our behalf. Jesus speaks the mysterious words about the coming of night which are a prophecy of his own hour of battle with darkness.

"As he said this, he spat on the ground and made clay of the spittle, saying to him, 'Go, wash in the pool of Siloam.' " Why this strange behavior? Jesus does not ask the young man if he wants to be granted his sight. This is an act of sheer grace.

One very simple interpretation of this event is that when the mud is put upon his eyes and Jesus instructs him to wash off the mud, the young man is eager to do so. Jesus has made it easier for the man to obey. Another possibility has been suggested: Jesus may have made clay as a further challenge to Sabbath observance. The spitting incident is itself offensive to devout Jews, who carefully avoided anything that might be thought of as magical. The Mishnaic document Sanhedrin (10:1) specifically includes spitting as one of the charms that are rejected as dangerous and magical. Jesus does not grant any teaching significance to the spitting act; therefore it is well for us to let the act simply stand as is.

John specifically names the pool as Siloam, which is located at the southern boundary of the city. It is this pool from which the basins of water are drawn and carried to the temple for the Feast of Tabernacles ceremonies. "Shiloah," the Hebrew word for Siloam, appears to be related to the Hebrew root word for "to send."

The man returns from the pool able to see. What follows is a sequence of fascinating dialogue in which two movements of attitude and experience occur. We watch this young man emerge from his bondage to darkness and his life as a beggar to the place where he is boldly able to carry on a discussion at a deep level about life and its meaning with the learned authorities. We note his increasing openness toward life and his eagerness to believe.

On the other side, the narrative portrays the cumulative antagonism and tightening circles of frustration in the case of the Pharisees who quiz the young man and his parents. Finally they throw him out of the temple precincts. "You were born in utter sin, and would you teach us?" (v. 24). This final sentence tells more about the learned men than the young man.

Jesus is not only the great physician, he is the pastor who finds this young man in order to confirm for him his discovery and disclose to him his messiahship. The narrative closes with a postscript conversation between the Pharisees and Jesus (vv. 39–41). The words of Jesus are not so much the words of judgment as they are words of invitation.

At the heart of this critical moment of self-discovery is a gift, and some of those who are standing by may be very close to receiving that gift. When the arrogant refusal to see begins to break down, relationships are then moved to a deeper level of communication, and truth is discovered.

In the parable of the shepherd,
Jesus draws together the themes
and meanings of his ministry.

21. The Good Shepherd
John 10:1-42

Chapter 10 begins with the Greek words *Amen, amen*. These are
not typically used by Jesus at the beginning of new discourses but
rather within discourses. (See 1:51; 3:3, 5; 5:24, 25; 6:25, 32, 52;
8:34, 58; 13:16, 70; 14:12.) Therefore we will interpret chapter 10 as
the continuation of the temple incident recorded in chapter 9.

The chapter begins with a brief proverb in verses 1-5. The Greek
word used is the word *paroimia*. In the Septuagint this word and
the word *parabolē* are both used interchangeably to translate the
Hebrew word *mashal*, which is used to describe all kinds of figurative language. The same word will be used in chapter 16:25: "I shall
no longer speak in figures." Parables and figurative speech are
used in John, but not so much in the short story sense, as in the
parables of Matthew, Mark and Luke, though John's figures have
the same overall purpose—that is, to teach by means of an illustration. A figure is presented by Jesus which the listener is able to understand by analogy to his own experience. Jesus spoke and taught
from a Hebrew point of view and not in the highly precise oratori-
cal tradition of the Greeks. He makes use of simple analogy, alle-
gory and short story parables as well as the didactic kind of teaching that we see in its dialogue form in John and in its distilled
epigrammatic form in Matthew and Mark and Luke. In this tenth
chapter we see several of these forms of teaching converge in a
single passage.

The proverb that Jesus tells in verses 1-4 draws several themes
together as only a parable is able to do. Note two main ingredients:
First, the parable begins with the image of a sheepfold; it has one
door; the gatekeeper allows in the true shepherd; the sheep know
the shepherd and the shepherd calls the sheep by name; the shepherd leads them and the sheep follow him. Then, the parable introduces the negative possibility. There is the stranger whom the

sheep will not follow because they do not recognize his voice. John tells us that those who heard the parable did not understand its meaning. Therefore, as with the parable of the wheat and the weeds in Matthew 13, Jesus explains it, gives meaning to several parts of the story line and, in fact, enlarges the story line. Let us attempt to trace the theme development as Jesus draws out several parts of the parable for his listeners:

(1) "I am the door of the sheep." Jesus is the entrance through which every truth, every teacher, and every disciple must enter. (In small mountain folds, the shepherd would often become the very door by sleeping across the opening to the fold.)

(2) All those themes and teachers that do not enter by this doorway are false. Jesus has, by this interpretation, made himself the very criterion of truth. He is teaching that every theme out of the past or in the present receives its meaning in terms of how it relates to the door that God has established. The Law of Moses must enter by this doorway. When it does not, as in the case of the adulterous woman brought to Jesus in chapter 8, it and its proponents are proved to be thieves and bandits seeking not the good of God's flock but its destruction and the destruction of the very door itself.

Jesus tests every prophet, teacher and teaching in terms of their relationship with the door. Even such apparently reverent language as the Pharisees used in their discussions with the young man born blind ("Give God the praise," 9:24)—words that sound devout but are really a disguise for false motives—even such religious language as that does not pass through the door and therefore is false. The criteria for the true prophet have been set forth. Jesus tells us that the purpose of his coming is so that the sheep may have life and have it abundantly.

(3) Jesus further develops his interpretation of the parable. He is not only the door but he is the shepherd too. "I am the excellent shepherd." The word *kalos*, translated "good" in the RSV, carries with it the sense of competent, excellent. Jesus is the shepherd who does not lose his sheep. We have witnessed this shepherd skill of Jesus in these opening chapters. Jesus found Nathanael; he found the woman at the well; he found the lonely man at Bethesda; he found the young man born blind—"Jesus heard that they had cast him out, and having found him he said . . . " (9:35).

But Jesus intends even more in the simile of the shepherd. He tells about the sacrifice that this shepherd will make in behalf of the sheep. "The good shepherd lays down his life for the sheep." He is not like the hired part-time worker who has less at stake and therefore takes fewer risks in the face of danger. Jesus is the shepherd who risks his very life for the sheep. He knows each one of the sheep by name and his sheep know him. Jesus is the shepherd who, of his own decision, lays down his life—not as a victim, because even in death his authority remains. In this context, Jesus here predicts his victory over death. Because his father has willed it, Jesus lays down his life and will "take it again." This sentence is the fullest and most open prophecy concerning his coming hour that we have heard to this point in the Gospel.

(4) Who are the sheep? In the perspective of the total context of this dialogue, it becomes clear that the sheep are the ones who hear the voice of the shepherd (v. 3). The sheep follow him (v. 4). They do not follow the false shepherds (v. 5). The very names of the sheep are known by the shepherd and they know him (v. 14). I do not accept Bultmann's thesis that John's use of the word *know* here is due to Gnostic influence. Jesus' teaching and storytelling in this parable with its allegorical treatment is dramatically and wholly Semitic. The emphasis on *name* is an example of just that Semitic kind of thinking. Sheepherders have named sheep for centuries.

Jesus adds to this portrayal a further description: "And I have other sheep, that are not of this fold; I must bring them also, and they will heed my voice. So there shall be one flock, one shepherd." This universal note greatly expands the parable. It clearly states in words what in fact Jesus Christ has been doing by action. He has welcomed into the shepherd's fold people from a wide cross section and sweep of background and nationality and along the whole social acceptance scale. What a list! From the distinguished Nicodemus to the beggar born blind—the Samaritan woman, the royal official.

The important theological point is that Jesus as the door and the shepherd is the one who invites the sheep into the fold. The only other criterion that matters is the willingness of the sheep to hear, to follow and to enter. In this parable, the freedom of the shepherd and the freedom of the sheep are both preserved. But the authority of the sheep to decide upon which other sheep are to be approved for entrance has been disallowed by the shepherd himself. If and when we as beloved sheep take that authority upon ourselves, we then become the shepherd, and in the terms of this parable it means that we have become false shepherds because we have chosen another door of entry than Jesus Christ and him alone. He is the only door. Therefore, racial tests for entry or nationalistic, tribal tests are against the parable. The only test we know of is how we stand with Jesus Christ himself. This is the only criterion.

Jesus decidedly does not teach that there are many shepherds and many flocks all journeying by separate paths to a great and holy destination. He is clear—there are many sheep from many places that he will draw together into the flock that belongs to the one shepherd.

John tells us that these words trigger a sharp division among the people. Some are profoundly impressed by Jesus' words and deeds and others remain baffled by it all. Still others feel that Jesus is possessed by a demon and is mad—they intend to stop listening. It is interesting how often in the history of mankind the charge of insanity has been used to disqualify the dangerous teacher. Alexander Solzhenitzyn as well as many other Russian intellectuals have been sentenced to mental hospitals in the Soviet Union. Because their thoughts are dangerous to the doctrines of the state, they are considered mad. Nowhere in John's Gospel are the opponents of Jesus and their arguments ridiculed by John. They are always seriously considered. This feature is especially true in relation to the theological objections to Jesus and his claims; in this setting we hear some of the most vital teaching about tests, especially in this tenth chapter. Jesus remains a difficult problem to solve for everyone around him.

Evidently the second part of the chapter (10:22–42) occurs later in the fall, toward December. John places this part of the dialogue during the time of the Feast of Dedication (Hanukkah). In continuing dialogue with people confused as to who Jesus really is, he gives one more additional insight into the sheep-shepherd figure. "I give them eternal life, and they shall never perish, and no one shall snatch them out of my hand" (v. 28).

Jesus' sheep possess a rich destiny of eternal life, and there are no bandits or predators able to destroy that destiny. Jesus is not teaching that there is something instinctive within us that is indestructible, such as the Greek idea of an immortal soul which is trapped within the mortal prison of our flesh. In that view, our essence has about itself its own immortal nature. For those who hold that view death is, therefore, only the destruction of the mortal outer shell. The soul has its own essential and immortal life. In such a case something about *me* is the basis of my hope. To be sure it is secret and mysterious, but still I in my mystical self am my own good news. In contrast to this, Jesus and his New Testament followers, are teaching a whole view of our nature. The gift of eternal life is essentially a relationship with the shepherd and the sheep—with us and the Lord. Therefore, it is eternal life for the whole self—body and soul. It is life seen as victory over death. Therefore, as this Gospel will make clear, the Christian hope is not a doctrine about our immortal soul but consists in our relationship with the good shepherd Jesus Christ, who does not lose his sheep— even in the valley of the shadow of death. The victory of that shepherd over death means that we will not ultimately perish. We are not the Gospel—Jesus is!

John continues to be careful to note the shape and direction of the various arguments posed against Jesus. In this incident Jesus' questioners have raised the central question: "It is not for a good work that we stone you but for blasphemy; because you, being a man, make yourself God" (v. 31). The answer of Jesus to this question is to shift the debate from the argument over words to the testing of action. Jesus shows by a skillful quotation from Psalm 82:6 that the word *God* is not the issue. Debates over language cannot be separated from events. Jesus' reply is very Hebraic and concrete. Its theological importance rests in the fact that Jesus always unites the *noetic* and the *ontic*, knowledge and being, the word and the event. They may not be separated.

With this dialogue the great midpart of the ministry of Jesus comes to its close in John's portrayal. Chapter 11 begins the final days of our Lord's ministry—his hour.

To the family of Mary, Martha and Lazarus, Jesus gives the great sign —the raising of Lazarus from the dead.

22. The Bethany Incident
John 11:1–44

John introduces his readers for the first time to three good friends of Jesus: Mary, Martha, and Lazarus. The text reminds the readers that it was Mary who anointed the Lord with ointment and wiped his feet with her hair. This sentence at the opening of chapter 11 is interesting in that John relates that very event in the next chapter (12:1–8). There is, therefore, no point in this identification for the purpose of this Gospel's narrative development, unless it is John's concern to identify the scene in Mark's Gospel in which Mark does not give Mary's name (Mark 14:3–9). I believe it is the most reasonable assumption to recognize this reference as one more indication that John is aware of the other Gospel writers, and that he makes the identification at this point to remind his readers of Mark's account. It is also an evidence of the earlier writing and circulation of Mark.

Luke is the only other Gospel writer who makes reference to Jesus' relationship with this family. Luke 10:38 tells of a visit by Jesus to the home of Mary and Martha. Therefore John's identifying statement gives us another evidence of how widely circulated the Gospel accounts were among the early churches. The other Gospels tell us that during Jesus' time at Jerusalem he spent his evenings at Bethany, a small village across the valley Kidron and some two miles from Jerusalem. It is John who tells in detail of the family with whom Jesus stayed.

The name Lazarus is the shortened form of Eleazar, which we know is a common name during the first century. The raising of Lazarus is given a very prominent position in John but is not mentioned in the other Gospels. This does not surprise us, however, because we have come to expect from John that he will especially discuss events which the other Gospels do not mention—i.e., the interview with the woman at the well, the marriage at Cana, Nicodemus, the man at the pool of Bethesda, the young man born blind. The Lazarus miracle is portrayed by John as being the crucial event that triggers the wrath of Jesus' opponents to the point that they agree to a deadly strategy against him. John here puts into place a major piece of the psychological puzzle: that is, how this teacher from Galilee could become so famous with the people to inspire the public show of affection on Palm Sunday and then, how such strong opposition could have coalesced to the point of agreement among basically dissimilar groups like the Sadducees and the Pharisees.

Jesus is across Jordan at Perea when the news comes to him from Mary and Martha of the illness of their brother Lazarus. Jesus answers the messengers, "This illness is not unto death; it is for the glory of God, so that the Son of God may be glorified." In only three places in John's Gospel does Jesus use the phrase "Son of God." One instance is John 5:25. In both of these instances, Jesus uses the term in an indirect way.

John tells us that Jesus loved Lazarus, yet he stays on at Perea. After two days he announces his plan to go to Judea. His disciples are wary because they already sense the menace that has grown since the close of the temple discourses. Jesus tells them of the death of Lazarus and they leave for Judea. Thomas the Twin comes into the Gospel narrative for the first time. His statement may be interpreted in one of two ways. "Let us also go, that we may die with him" is a statement either of courage in the face of danger, or of warning and melancholy fearfulness; in either case, Thomas the realist is aware of the extent of the danger.

When they arrive at Bethany, they discover that Lazarus is dead and buried. In first-century Jewish death practice, the body is buried without embalming on the day of death and the mourning lasts for thirty days.

Martha, the practical and no-nonsense sister (Luke 10:38), comes to meet Jesus. Mary, the more emotional and fragile one, stays at the house in mourning. Martha has strong faith in Jesus. Her words are clipped, definite: "Lord, if you had been here my brother would not have died. And even now I know that whatever you ask from God, God will give you." Her words are strong, but she does not realize their full meaning and possibility. Jesus answers her: "Your brother will rise again." Martha answers, "I know that he will rise again in the resurrection at the last day." Martha agrees to Jesus' words, but not in any way expecting what Jesus means by them in the immediate situation. She replies with her hope in the future resurrection.

As a part of their teaching, the Pharisees had developed a firm eschatalogical belief in the resurrection of the body. This doctrine is rooted in Daniel 12:2 and was widely accepted by the common people by the first century, though denied by the Sadducees. An intense controversy raged between Sadducees and Pharisees over this doctrine (Mark 12:8; Acts 23:8).

The answer of Jesus Christ to Martha's doctrine is the most moving of all the great "I am" affirmations of Jesus: "I am the resurrection and the life, he who believes in me, though he die, yet shall he live, and whoever lives and believes in me shall never die." Jesus is not the giver of victory somewhere in the obscure future. He is the victory over death in the actual present. Because of this amazing sentence, we today do not need to develop elaborate theories about resurrection or the future. We have the living, reigning Lord of past, present, future, who is himself the victory over death here and now. Jesus goes on to say that those who trust in him share in his victory, both in the future and in the present. Martha answers with her own confession of faith in Jesus as Lord. She gives no clue by her words or actions that she expects the Lord to raise Lazarus from the dead. It is enough that she trusts simply in Jesus himself.

Luke has only pictured for us a busy and preoccupied Martha, but John has put this amazing woman into her true and proper focus. In the midst of overwhelming grief and personal loss, she confesses her faith in Jesus Christ as the Lord.

Martha then goes back to the house to find her sister Mary and bring her to meet Jesus, and he is overcome by Mary's sorrow, "Jesus wept." This shortest verse in the Bible gives us one more insight into the tenderness and human warmth of Jesus. The unaffected and spare language in which John tells this account gives us confidence in the truthfulness of the event itself. "Jesus wept"—not a phantom Jesus in a story about him drawn up by the early church designed by creative writers to tell the kerygma of their Easter faith. The early church does not create myths about the love of Jesus. Jesus loved—and without the early church storyteller's help. All that the church needed to do was to tell honestly what really happened. We do not need gospel folk myths to assure us that Jesus Christ cares about our concrete existence. The simple record of what he said and did, and the brief glimpse we have here as to how he felt—these are what we need. The persuasive force of the New Testament Gospels rests not in amazing and skillfully told stories but in the earnestness and the feel of truthfulness which focus our attention upon the acts and words of Jesus himself.

Jesus then commands that the stone be moved away from the tomb. Martha, practical and realistic, urges against it, "Lord, by this time there will be an odor, for he has been dead four days." Finally she trusts in the promise of Jesus and agrees to his instructions. Jesus prays and then shouts, "Lazarus, come out." Lazarus, still bound with burial cloths around his body, emerges. The people unbind him. Jesus has given a sign of the reality of his authority—even over death itself.

This very specific and particular victory of the authority of Jesus Christ over death in favor of a man called Lazarus has profound theological and discipleship implications. He stands before and beyond the limits we know as birth and death. Even the death of this one human being is bounded within the strong and loving reign of Jesus of Nazareth. We should not, therefore, be surprised at the outburst of total amazement among those who knew for a fact that Lazarus had died, as well as confusion and doubt among those who only heard second-hand of this event.

But an even greater destiny lay before Lazarus. This victory over the tomb at Bethany is itself a sign of the greater conquest to come. Lazarus will die some day as all men and women die. Therefore, his resurrection at Bethany is not as great a miracle as the one that all humanity is offered in the gospel of Jesus Christ, "Whoever believes . . . should not perish but have eternal life" (John 3:16).

The coalition against Jesus is now formed, and a deadly decision is made.

23. Conspiracy
John 11:45–57

The incident at Bethany encourages the faith of the disciples and greatly broadens the circle of believers. We are now better able to appreciate the reason for the great crowds on Palm Sunday, and the new optimism that for a few days will stir up the twelve disciples.

But this very sign, happening so close to Jerusalem, and so completely unbelievable when reported to others, also has the effect of hardening the opposition to Jesus. In order to form a coalition of theologically dissimilar groups, they must find cause for the coalition in a concern that they all equally share. Whereas the Pharisees we met earlier in the Gospel wanted to talk about theological concerns, they now find themselves driven into alliance with their long-time foes, the priestly Sadducee party. "If we let him go on thus, every one will believe in him, and the Romans will come and destroy both our holy place and our nation." They fear unrest or perhaps insurrection. Rome had demonstrated that their policy throughout the empire was not to interfere in religious controversy or to tamper with religious practice. Josephus gives examples of this policy. However, anarchy or people-movement unrest they would not tolerate, as the events of A.D. 60–70 attest. It is therefore the fame and popularity of Jesus among a growing number of Judeans that now poses the problem.

Caiaphas, who was high priest from A.D. 18 to 36, speaks the words that unite the coalition. They are cynical and opportunistic, but the crafty Caiaphas makes them sufficiently lofty and religious to win over the Pharisees who, more than the Sadducees, are deeply religious. Pharisees think in religious not political terms. "Men never delight in doing evil as much as if they can do it for religious reasons" (Blaise Pascal, *Pensées*, no. 894).

This event carries within it important warnings to all devout

105

people. There is a tendency within movements to create a body of approved language and phrases which, as they are quoted and used skillfully, may become an effective screen able to hide darker motives. It is assumed that the speech is sound and true as long as the approved vocabulary is used. In fact, the words may mask totally corrupt purposes. This is why in Christian theology and ethics *word* and *work*, *means* and *ends* are inseparable. Approved themes may be quoted and unpopular ones avoided, but that still does not mean that a teaching is biblical and Christian. It may be Caiaphas saying just the words he needs to say in order to deceive sincere, frightened Pharisees.

His words achieve the goal he has in mind. The conspiracy is set in motion. John makes one very important theological comment about Caiaphas's words: "it is expedient for you that one man should die for the people." John reflects upon this cynical statement: "He did not say this of his own accord, but being high priest that year he prophesied that Jesus should die for the nation, and not for the nation only, but to gather into one the children of God who are scattered abroad." Little did Caiaphas realize that his words were in fact deeply prophetic—that by these words of conspiracy he also would be bearing witness to who Jesus is and to Jesus' redeeming sacrifice for Israel. But John goes further than Caiaphas. John realizes that Jesus' sacrifice has worldwide significance. John favors this sort of family language to express the goal of Jesus' ministry rather than the kingdom language which we see in the Synoptics.

Now the scene is set for the hour in which all of this prophecy will converge.

*When Jesus enters Jerusalem, the
people recognize who he is—their
king.*

24. The People's King
John 12:1–19

The next event is one that Mark and Matthew also have included in their Gospels (Mark 14:3–9; Matt. 26:6–13). There is an incident in Luke's Gospel (Luke 7:36–34) which is similar only in that Jesus' feet are anointed, but in that instance by the tears of an unnamed woman. We may, therefore, conclude that Luke's account is of a separate incident.

The comparison between John's narrative and that of Matthew / Mark is very interesting. John, who is aware of the other accounts (see comment on 11:2), may here in his own account—if they are of the same event—be making some significant and clarifying comments. He identifies Mary as the woman who anointed Jesus' feet. He places this event prior to Palm Sunday. He identifies Judas Iscariot as the one who rebuked the act of Mary. One possibility suggested by some interpreters is that Judas, who is identified as son of Simon, might be a member of the family of Mary, Martha, and Lazarus. Mark tells us that the event occurred in the house of Simon the leper in Bethany. John makes no mention of Simon except that Judas Iscariot is called Judas son of Simon (John 6:71).

Judas is critical of the use of the costly nard ointment. He tells us that its value is equal to the equivalent of three hundred days' work for a laborer. By today's standards, at $3.00 per hour, that amounts to $9,000.00. However, there is no rebuke of Mary for the informality and surprising act of untying her hair in public—something a woman does not usually do in first-century practice. If it is true, as some tradition has concluded, that the woman in Luke 7 who untied her hair in grief and thanksgiving to wipe her own tears from the feet of Jesus is Mary of Magdala, could it be that this Mary at Bethany may know and love Mary Magdalene as a sister in Christ and by this act now be showing her identification with the other Mary? Costly ointments are not usually put upon the

107

feet of a person, and perhaps this, together with other more secret reasons, angers Judas. Only in John's Gospel do we discover that Judas is the keeper of the disciples' money. Jesus knows the secrets of Judas, but the crowd will not learn them from him. Like Caiaphas, Judas has used ethically impressive words to disguise a hidden purpose. Instead of challenging Judas, Jesus simply endorses Mary's act as "beautiful" (Matthew's phrase) and prophetic in that it points to his death. Her act has become a sign given by a believer to who Jesus is.

Jesus has interrupted the attempt of one disciple to disqualify the worship of another disciple. Christians express their worship of Jesus Christ in different ways, and Jesus here has granted a generous theological framework within which that worship may be expressed. Pragmatic and practical people have often been unable to understand the artistic and sensitive. But each has a mandate that is valid when it is subject to the authority of the Gospel of Jesus Christ. Jesus is so sure of himself and of his authority that one of the marks of that authority is the freedom he grants to those around him. He enables each disciple to express his or her own personality. The weeping Mary sorrowing at the death of her brother Lazarus is not scolded for failing to come out with Martha to meet Jesus. Nor is Martha put down for her natural and practical hesitation when Jesus instructs the people to open Lazarus's grave. Now her sister Mary is free to be herself and express what she feels.

The rebuke of Judas may supply a very important clue to the understanding of this enigmatic figure. His words about the poor, though perhaps a cover up of bad motives, as John concludes, may also fit together with a possible personality profile of this man. Is he a Zealot? Is he from a privileged family? He knows the value of a luxury item such as imported nard. Is Judas a nationalist who breaks with Jesus because of his own disappointment with him?

Luke tells us that just prior to this time in Bethany, Jesus had called the wealthy tax collector Zaccheus down from a tree in order to stay as a guest in his house (Luke 19). Luke says that everyone, disciples included, were shocked by Jesus' identification with such a man. "They all murmured," he says. Is that the place where Judas writes off the ministry of Jesus as irrelevant and meaningless as far as his own goals and burdens are concerned? And now this wasteful and wealthy display!

Judas is disappointed by Jesus, and perhaps his later betrayal of Jesus is stirred up from this disillusionment. Certainly, when Jesus on Palm Sunday throws away every advantage to launch a genuine "people's movement," Judas might then conclude that the Jesus he had loved had changed. Perhaps this, together with other motivations and temptations, causes Judas to betray his best friend.

John makes it clear that the immediate reason for the great crowds on Palm Sunday is the miracle of the raising of Lazarus. He also makes the point that Lazarus himself is marked for death by the chief priests. This may be their plan, but in a few days, when Jesus himself is in their grasp, they will evidently lose interest in the persecution of Lazarus. We have no record in the biblical witness of his martyrdom. It is Jesus who is to be the Redeemer, and as the Redeemer he will take the place of all mankind.

In J. R. R. Tolkien's *Fellowship of the Ring* (the first volume of *The Lord of the Rings* trilogy), the band of journeyers are trapped deep in the heart of the mountains at the bridge of Khazad-Dum by the dark shadow, the Balrog, mighty lord of the abyss. "Its streaming mane kindled, and blazed behind it. In its right hand was a blade like a stabbing tongue of fire; in its left it held a whip of many thongs." Only their leader, the wizard Gandalf, is able to stand up to this foe. "The Balrog stepped forward slowly on to the bridge, and suddenly it drew itself up to a great height, and its wings were spread from wall to wall; but still Gandalf could be seen, glimmering in the gloom; he seemed small, and altogether alone: grey and bent, like a wizened tree before the onset of a storm" (pp. 344, 345).

In the ensuing battle, Gandalf defeats the Balrog. But as the bridge cracks and the Balrog begins to fall, his whip catches hold of Gandalf's leg and pulls him down with him into the abyss. Gandalf faces this terrifying foe, and by giving his life, others are set free to escape to safety.

So Jesus Christ must face the deepest abyss of all time, alone. The plots and intrigue of priests and kings are the very real ingredients of a much greater battle. No one among the disciples' band will be able to stand at this final bridge. Only Jesus is able.

On the day of Jesus' entry into Jerusalem, the people are unaware of the intrigue among the powerful in Jerusalem. They greet Jesus as king. Each of the Gospels tells of the entry into Jerusalem. John's narrative is briefer than the others. Palm branches are used for the processions during the Feast of Tabernacles and were also used by Judas Maccabbeas in the ceremony of the Rededication of the Temple more than a hundred years earlier. Palm fronds would be a sign of praise and celebration which come naturally out of the people's life. All of the Gospels agree that the people called out the words of Psalm 118. This Psalm is the cry for help to the Lord and is used as a part of the celebration Psalms for the Feasts of Tabernacles, Dedication, and Passover. The word *Hosanna* means "Help us please," and is used as a praise word at the Tabernacles feast. The text records that Jesus rode into the city upon a young ass and so fulfilled the prophecy of Zechariah 9:9/14:4.

Jesus' entry into Jerusalem is a study in contrasts. Since Passover is to be held that week, the people of Jerusalem have probably witnessed the entry into their city of Herod and his entourage. This very wealthy man usually lived away from Jerusalem; however, at times of the great feasts he would make an appearance. Pilate as governor would usually stay on the coast at Caesarea, but he also must be in Jerusalem during the celebrations of the Jews. A Roman procession is dramatic and splendid; the great golden Roman eagle leads the way, followed by the pennants of Rome, the Roman soldiers and the chariots. The time of feasts are occasions for such drama and for the show of omnipotent Roman presence.

Now Jesus enters the city—on a donkey; the crowds of people make up the difference on Palm Sunday. They sense who Jesus Christ is. There is the shock of recognition on that day, and Jesus is honored by the people. In Luke's account of Palm Sunday, he records that the Pharisees challenged Jesus for accepting the praise of the people. " 'Teacher, rebuke your disciples.' He answered, 'I tell you, if these were silent, the very stones would cry out' " (Luke 19:39–40). Jesus is the people's king on Palm Sunday and they agree to it, proclaim it.

However, the Lord makes a profound point in his reply to the Pharisees. He *is the* king, and were the people to become silent, were they to cease their recognition (and they will within the week), he would still be king. He is objectively king as well as subjectively: if they cease their worship, the rocks will cry out. The lordship of Jesus Christ does not depend upon the acknowledgment of the people. In the Gospel accounts, the disciples' faith does not make Christ Lord. Their faith is a response to the fact that he is already Lord. But faith is not absolute or static, as the events of holy week will show. Faith is a growing, with ups and downs, a journey demanding continuing responses of discipleship. Only God himself and his speech—Jesus Christ—is absolute.

This fraility of our faith does not discount or erase the wonder and significance of Palm Sunday. On this day the people have made a genuine discovery of who is their Lord, and they say it out loud. John quotes the reaction of the Pharisees to this praise: " 'You see that you can do nothing; look, the world has gone after him' " (John 12:19).

Theologically we recognize in this incident the two great ingredients of faith: (1) The objective reality of who Jesus Christ is as Lord, which has its own integrity and reality quite apart from the reaction of mankind pro or con. Jesus Christ is Lord whether we like it or not. He is the prior fact and reason for our faith. (2) The second ingredient is the trust in Christ which is ours to decide and experience. Great crowds on Palm Sunday worshiped Jesus Christ (in fact, it is that show of the people's affection that speeded the conspiracy to definite action against Jesus). But five days later the crowd rejected Jesus. Since *faith* is a freedom word in the New Testament, it therefore wavers. God's decision to preserve that freedom of ours is the source of both our sorrow and our joy.

In theological terms, we must be sure to keep the two ingredients together and in the order of their true sequence. We should be wary of excessive subjectivity which is eloquent about the action of our faith and yet "speechless as to *what* we may believe" (see Karl Barth, *Dogmatics in Outline*, p. 15).

At the same moment, faith is ours to express and risk, but not as a general truth that universally applies but never demands our obedience. The World Council of Churches at its convening assembly in Amsterdam adopted a simple formula of faith that states, "We are a fellowship of churches that believe in Jesus Christ our Lord. . . ." At the New Delhi Assembly this formula was changed to read, "We are a fellowship of churches that confess Jesus Christ the Lord as God and Saviour. . . ." The New Delhi formula keeps the two ingredients in sharp focus—Jesus is *our* Lord. That is true. But even more. He is *the* Lord in whom we believe. His lordship is independent of our praise though he deserves our praise.

Jesus says that the way to the kingdom is through his own death, and that by dying he will win the victory over death and the devil.

25. A Hard Parable
John 12:20-50

"Now among those who went up to worship at the feast were some Greeks" (12:20).

The worries of the Pharisees are fulfilled immediately in this very next scene. Non-Jews, probably proselytes, that is, Gentiles who are strongly attracted by the purity of Jewish monotheism and yet have not become Jews (through the rite of circumcision), ask to see Jesus. When they meet him, he affirms the arrival of the moment that this Gospel has watched for since his first sign at Cana. "Jesus answered them, 'The hour has come for the Son of man to be glorified.'" Here we have one more instance of the fact that Jesus' goal is not to fulfill nationalistic objectives of first-century messianic hope; the whole world is the real context of his ministry and victory.

"Amen, amen, I say to you, unless a grain of wheat falls into the earth and dies, it remains alone; but if it dies, it bears much fruit." This brief parable with its melancholy theme seems incongruous in the glorious and thrilling setting of the triumphal entry. Jesus knows that the faith shown by the people in him must now be profoundly tested. He predicts victory but not without defeat. Jesus turns to his followers and speaks very hard words to the joyous marchers, many of whom can taste the kingdom in their mouths. The strong words of this parable —*"hates* his life" "falls into the earth and *dies"*—are used to make the choice sharp and impossible in our own strength and on the basis of our own ego motivational resources.

Jesus is troubled. He prays that the Father will "glorify thy name." John tells us of a voice, which the people do not understand—some hear a voice, others hear thunder. The voice speaks, "I have glorified it and will glorify it again" (12:28). John does not give us the account of the Mount of Transfiguration where a voice from heaven confirms the identity of Jesus to three of his disciples, but he does include this incident which is omitted in the Synoptics.

Following this witness to himself as the Christ, Jesus speaks again: "Now is the judgment of this world, now shall the ruler of this world be cast out." These phrases do not appear in the other Gospels. Paul uses the same imagery as a reference to Satan (in 1 Cor. 2:6–8; 2 Cor. 4:4; Eph. 2:2; 4:12).

The Bible recognizes the existence of Satan and portrays him as personal, moral will against the will of God. Theologically, the existence of Satan in the spiritual realm of creation is the result of God's decision to provide real freedom and therefore the possibility of choice against his will as well as choice for his will. There is power in deciding against God's will, and Jesus here refers to that power. We know from our own experience that when we decide against God's will—against his righteousness—on even our human scale, we may experience a surge of power in our lives and relationships. When we are not bound and slowed down by the ethical restraints of justice and love, we are at first able to advance any cause quickly and powerfully. We operate by a short-cut ethic because we are free from the authority of God. But this power is the power of the destroyer, and though it disguises itself with many apparently righteous masks, the result of its power is always deadly.

Jesus now announces that what is at stake in his hour is a battle on a far larger scale than the meager controversies of temple politics. Jesus is establishing his kingdom over against the deadly reign of the prince of the world. Two surprises now confront us.

(1) The first surprise is Jesus' explanation of the way that Satan will be overthrown. Somehow, Satan will be conquered through Jesus' death. Jesus states this as if there were no other way. The power of evil is disarmed as its fury is taken full force.

(2) The second surprise is Jesus' claim that through his death he will draw all people to himself. Not the triumphal king but the suffering servant will draw the world to his reign. His listeners are not prepared for these words of humiliation. They expect the Messiah to reign without humiliation. They think of themselves as the suffering servants and that their king is above humiliation. This majestic expectation now becomes a major roadblock to faith. The disciples are willing to see Christ win but not to suffer shame.

At this point in the narrative, John reaches into the prophecies of Isaiah 53:1 and 6:9–10 to explain how the people fail to really trust in Jesus Christ and to accept his messiahship as he marks out his course. John quotes both texts: the first expresses wonder and amazement at the beginning of the portrayal of the suffering servant passage in Isaiah 53, and is quoted verbatim from the Septuagint. The Isaiah 6:9–10 quotation also appears in the other Gospels, but there it is Jesus who speaks it (Matthew 13:13–15) at an earlier point in his ministry. Here it is John who makes use of it as an Old Testament prophecy which is in effect a source for the statement John made in the prologue. "He came to his own home, and his own people received him not" (1:11). In this quotation John takes the liberty of offering his own free translation of the Isaiah 6:9–10 text, one that is slightly different from the Septuagint and Hebrew text.

Jesus Christ's words are permanent and have full binding authority. Upon this note chapter 12 concludes.

26. The Servant Lord

John 13:1–30

When the people think of Messiah they think of a king like David, but when Jesus Christ, who is the Messiah, comes he is a servant. There are no great mass meetings, no torchlight parades well orchestrated by political organizers. The advantage Jesus has gained on Palm Sunday from a mass movement standpoint he quickly leaves behind as unimportant to him. Instead, as we noted in chapter 12, he continues the great theme he began in the Good Shepherd teaching of chapter 10. Jesus tells the people that he is to be the suffering Lord who lays down his life and who is lifted up in the humiliation of death. In this way which we find so strange to our thinking, Jesus tells his listeners that the Devil will be defeated.

John now moves his narration to Thursday of Holy Week, leaving to the other Gospel writers the task of giving to us the events of Monday, Tuesday, Wednesday.

On the evening of Palm Sunday, Jesus has spoken about the servant Lord. Now on Thursday evening his acts show in concrete form what his words mean.

John alone of the Gospel writers describes the event of the washing of the disciples' feet. He begins his narrative with the interpretive statement about the inner feelings of Jesus as he came to this moment. At the opening of this commentary, I observed that John's Gospel is unique in this regard. It contains more of this kind of interior and intimate narration than we find in Matthew, Mark or Luke. These features in the document, I believe, add internal evidence to support the traditions of the church fathers which attribute this Gospel to the disciple John himself. Such statements which purport to supply the thoughts and inner motivations of Jesus are the kind of writing we expect either from a writer very close to the person described and therefore in a privi-

115

leged position to know, or from someone writing very far from the event, long after any possible living witnesses are around. Only then would such intimate detail about feelings and attitude be possible without fear of contradiction. This is a historical rule of thumb. If living witnesses are still available, writers must then show restraint when describing such inner detail, for fear that they will be challenged to prove their accuracy by quotations and documents—unless they are themselves close enough to the subject matter to warrant such detail.

Following John's description of the inner feelings of Jesus, he makes the brief observation that Judas Iscariot has in his heart now fallen to Satan's temptation to betray Jesus. Then John narrates his own portrayal of the Last Supper. John is definite about the fact that this meal is held *before* the feast of Passover. At this point John has clarified a problem that arises from the chronology of Holy Week as portrayed in the Synoptic accounts. They speak of a *passover meal:* "So Jesus sent Peter and John saying, 'Go and prepare the passover for us, that we may eat it' " (Luke 22:8). John is specific in his dating. Therefore we conclude: "On Thursday evening, the 14th of Nisan by the official calendar, the day before Passover, Jesus ate with his disciples a meal that had passover characteristics" (Brown, *Gospel According to John,* p. 556).

After the supper, Jesus begins to wash the feet of the disciples. The other Gospels tell us that the mood of the disciples at the beginning of this supper is competitive. "A dispute also arose among them, which of them was to be regarded as the greatest" (Luke 22: 24). Has Luke given us a clue as to why this task had been forgotten? We must remember that though Jesus senses the danger before him, the disciples are still glowing in the wonder of the people's praise. They now feel victory—not danger—in their bones. They are in the mood to argue about the plans for ruling the kingdom and are not in the mood to serve each other. Research into first-century Jewish custom points up that footwashing is not a task required of a Jewish slave. People wash their own feet upon entering a home, with water supplied by their host. Footwashing is a voluntary act, not a mandatory one. What we see, therefore, in the disciples at the opening of this supper is not a breach of laws or rules of conduct; rather we see men who are relating to each other and even toward their teacher in a minimal way.

Jesus washed the disciples' feet, ending with Peter the acknowledged leader. Is Peter offended and embarrassed by the act of Jesus? His feelings burst out when his turn comes, and he says: " 'Lord, do you wash my feet?' Jesus answered him, 'What I am

doing you do not know now, but afterward you will understand.'
Peter said to him, 'You shall never wash my feet.' " There is a complex mixture of feelings and meanings in Peter's words. (1) By
these words he may be saying to Jesus, "Lord, you are the teacher,
I am the disciple and I do not want your *honor* compromised by
this act." (2) A more subtle feeling that may also be present is
Peter's own reticence at being served by the one he has so
idealized. (3) Or Peter may be one who finds it hard to receive. Receiving heightens a person's sense of vulnerability, whereas Peter
is a rocklike person.

In each case Peter's understanding of the meaning of the glory of
Christ and his feelings as to how that lordship should act are in the
process of being permanently altered. Those closest to Jesus have
already formed their own ideal picture of Jesus Christ and his
lordship, and they are not easily able to see it changed. This ideal
perception of Christ has influenced their self-understanding and
interpersonal feelings too. They argue about greatness on the basis
of definitions that they have formed. They have been with Jesus
and have heard him teach, but they still do not really know him
nor have they really heard him.

Perhaps Peter rejects the footwashing because he refuses to
allow even Jesus to tamper with his own triumphal vision of
Christ. Peter's theological feelings have very deep psychological
implications. He is a strong and courageous leader himself, and he
now finds it humiliating and a threat to his own self-consciousness
to accept a simple and lowly act. By his commanding words Peter
proves his leadership and his superiority over the other disciples
who were too shy to protest. His words honor Christ on the surface,
but at their core they honor Peter more. He is the one who needs
nothing, unlike the other disciples who need all of the strokes they
can get. This is a basic danger in the superlative words of much of
what we call worship. The very words of praise on our lips may be
in reality great barriers we build up to keep the Lord away from
our true self. They protect our vulnerability like flattery does when
we honor people we secretly fear.

But as Jesus was too good and too strong for the evasive language of Nicodemus or the woman at the well, so he will not be put
off by Peter's words. He is a very good shepherd; he proved to
those lonely people that he could find them and now he finds
Peter. He knows that Peter more than anything else, more even
than his own pretentions to greatness, wants to belong to him. Our
Lord's words to Peter are sensitive and strong and good: "If I do
not wash you, you have no part in me." His words break through

every proud defense, and we hear from Peter the warm and joyous enthusiasm that has endeared this man to us: "Lord, not my feet only but also my hands and my head." The beginning of a new era in Peter's discipleship has started. He will collapse within hours, but Jesus' prediction will hold: "but afterwards you will understand."

Jesus does not wash Peter's head and hands because what he has done is sufficient. He meant the footwashing event as a sign, and now he interprets it to them. He calls it an example of the servant role that they as his disciples are to take toward each other.

Jesus then acknowledges that he is aware of the betrayal that faces him. John tells the readers that as Judas left the room the other disciples, except for Peter and John himself, did not realize why Judas had gone out.

"And it was night." John adds this terse notation of time to his narrative of Holy Week events, but it is more than that. The nighttime he tells of will represent for all ages a deeper, more harrowing nighttime of the soul. But it will also be a night out of which hope is born.

27. The Lonely Valley
John 13:31–38

Now begins a long discourse given by Jesus to his disciples fol lowing the footwashing at the Last Supper and extending up until his arrest in the garden of Gethsemane. John devotes more than three full chapters in the text as we have it (chapter 13:31 through chapter 16). The teaching is intense and personal. This final discourse begins with a repetitious use of the word *glory*. Peter had just learned that what he thought the word meant was very wide of the mark. Now Jesus will use that word that has to do with the very presence of God himself as the opening invocation of this nighttime teaching. The hour of glory is here.

Following this invocation, the first theme that Jesus shares has to do with the fact that the pathway now before him he must face alone. "Where I am going you cannot come." The disciples do not understand what Jesus means by these words, and throughout this evening discourse a major question on their minds will be the mystery contained in them. Jesus assures them that later on they will understand and indeed follow him. Now, however the way is for Jesus alone.

Peter again protests with brave words, "Lord, why cannot I follow you now? I will lay down my life for you." Jesus answers Peter. " . . . I say to you, the cock will not crow, till you have denied me three times." Before sunrise, Jesus tells Peter, I know that even you will crumble because of the heavy weight of this hard night. By these words Jesus has done a beautiful thing for Peter. They are spoken to Peter at the opening of a great discourse in which Jesus will assure his disciples of his love for them. This means that before dawn of the next day when, in fact, an exhausted and frightened Peter has panicked and denied Jesus, he will then remember that Jesus had foreseen his failure. Before Jesus speaks the words of assurance and the strong expressions of his love that are recorded in these chapters, he knew of the fraility of his disciples and of his chief disciple. He knows their limits, and therefore these words are not severe and cynical but the raw material out of which a new foundation of self-worth and faith will later be built for Peter. They are the realistic words of the Shepherd who knows the strengths and weaknesses of his disciples and yet loves them.

They cannot follow Jesus—that is the point, and the prophecy concerning Peter's denial should be seen in that larger context. The theological importance of Jesus' words should not be missed. Only Jesus Christ is to be the world's Redeemer. The disciples are not! It is that basic. Jesus does not expect those men or any men or women to redeem the world. When we become confused at this vital point, we fall into the kind of theological error that causes harm to ourselves and to those around us. Both emotionally and theologically, the greatest fact about the gospel is that *we* are not the gospel. It is not our bravery or our greatness that is the redeeming victory over death, sin and the devil. It is Jesus Christ and he alone who is the Redeemer, and our discipleship tasks flow out of his act not ours. It is well for the first-century disciples and for us today that Peter falls and falls so hard! It is well that all of our hereos have clay feet so that we do not ask too much of them.

Fyodor Dostoevsky has movingly brought us into the heart of this basic understanding of the source of our faith in *The Brothers Karamazov*. Alyosha has learned much of the gospel from his beloved father in the faith, the monk, Zosima. When Fr. Zosima dies, the disciples of this great Christian man expect that since he is so great in his faith his body will not develop the odor of death. They had the superstition that the greater the man the longer after death his body could lie in state without the smell of decay. To the amazement of the devout Alyosha, his teacher's body begins to smell within hours after his death. Immediately on the rumor of this news, the monks in the monastery who were jealous of Zosima explain away his true greatness and now charge him with fraud and secret sins. Alyosha is crushed by the fall of his hero. But this superstitiously inspired failure does not become the defeat of Zosima's true greatness as a servant of Christ—it becomes the defeat of a superstition and a false criterion. Alyosha needed this shattering collapse of a false hope so that his life might be established upon the true hope.

Zosima, like Peter, is not the gospel. Both are witnesses to the gospel. The triumphalism that seeks to trivialize our faith by turning our attention to heroic men or women, past or present, as if they held secret powers in themselves and in their faith, is a false and dangerous pathway. We do not find it in the New Testament. The heroes of the New Testament, both before and after the victory of Easter and Pentecost, are all ordinary folk who know the taste of fear, regret, failure, selfishness and mistakes, but they have accepted the love of Jesus Christ in their lives and they are growing in that love. They are not redeemers; they are the ones like all the others who also need to be redeemed. They are not the Lord, they believe in the Lord. They are not gospel, they bear witness to the gospel.

How will the world know them? Jesus at the very opening of this great discourse gives a one-sentence answer that he will later explain in depth: "A new commandment I give to you, that you love one another; even as I have loved you." This is to be the mark of identification—not that Peter and the others are braver than the world. Jesus cuts off the brave promises of Peter.

Where Jesus is going no disciple is able to follow. The scope of that battle is too vast.

28. "In My Father's House"
John 14:1-14

Following the prophetic statement to Peter about his own impending denial, Jesus speaks words of hope: "Let not your hearts be thrown into confusion." The word translated "troubled" by the RSV, *tarassein*, is the word used earlier in 13:21 to describe Jesus' own feelings about the betrayal of Judas. It is a strong word that means "shudder," "thrown into confusion." Jesus will use the word again in 14:27: "Peace I leave you . . . let not your hearts be thrown into confusion." (It is also used in 1 Pet. 3:14.)

How can it be possible for Peter and the other disciples not to be troubled? Jesus' answer is: "Believe in God, believe also in me." Here the simple word *believe* carries the sense of trust; "Put your weight down upon the faithfulness of God and the faithfulness of his *Word* made flesh."

"In my father's house are many dwelling places." Jesus assures his disciples and all who will ever trust him that the goal of our lives is to dwell in the presence of God. This noun translated "rooms" (RSV) or "mansions" (KJV) is the word *monē*. In its verbal forms it will become a key part of the faith vocabulary of Jesus recorded in chapter 15; in that chapter its decisive usage by Jesus helps us to discover what he means by its use here in chapter 14. As a verb it is translated "remain" or "abide." "Abide in me and I in you. . . . If you abide in me and my words abide in you . . . " (John 15). Don't be confused, Jesus assures his disciples, because as you put your weight upon my trustworthiness you will find a safe abiding place.

"I go to prepare a place for you," Jesus continues. The language he uses is relationship language, and that is the essential clue to understanding what he means within this whole Thursday evening dialogue and high priestly prayer of chapter 17. He is not saying, "In my father's house are many temporary stations of rest enroute

122

to a final destination." This is how the early church fathers originally interpreted the word *monē*—as "a station on the pathway to God." This understanding sometimes resulted in the theory that the "soul in its ascent passes through stages wherein it is gradually purified of all that is material." (See Brown, *Gospel According to John* pp. 618, 619.) Here is an instance where the best meaning of a word is defined by the way it is subsequently used elsewhere in the document. It is clear that *monē* (and the verb forms related to it) is intended to communicate the sure relationship the disciples have in Christ. (See also this word later in this chapter, v. 33.) This is why they need not be troubled. Though Peter's hand will tire and loosen its grip upon Jesus, Jesus' hand will not lose its hold upon Peter. Jesus is urging Peter and the disciples to trust in the faithfulness of God so that when failure comes they will turn to Christ for help and not to emptiness.

Jesus promises his disciples that he is the one who stands at the future of their lives as he now stands with them in the present of their lives.

Thomas asked a question: "Lord, we do not know where you are going; how can we know the way?" Jesus' answer is one of the most memorable of all sentences. It is the great summary of his Yahweh affirmations: "I am the way, and the truth, and the life, no one comes to the Father, but by me"—"except through me." Jesus is not threatening or bragging or warning. He simply states the truth.

I am the *way*. By that word Jesus reminds his disciples of *the door* he had told them of in the proverb of John 10. "I am the door of the sheepfold" (10:7).

I am the *truth*. Jesus reminds them of what he had said in the temple after the incident when the woman caught in adultery was brought to him for his judgment. "I am the light of the world; he who follows me will not walk in darkness, but will have the light of life" (8:12).

I am the *life*. Jesus reminds them of his words to the crowd after the feeding of the multitudes, and of his word to Martha. "I am the bread of life; he who comes to me shall not hunger, and he who believes in me shall never thirst." "I am the resurrection and the life."

"Now you know the Father and have seen him"—experienced him concretely, Jesus tells his disciples (v. 17). But Philip still wants more visual assurance. His words are earnest, yet there is in them the flavor of the temptation of Jesus by Satan as recorded in Matthew and Luke. "Lord, show us the Father, and we shall be satisfied." Jesus answers with a rebuke of Philip and a rejection of his request for more proofs: "He who has seen me has seen the Father."

We are now at the radical center of the Christian gospel. We believe that Almighty God himself—the ultimate "I am" behind all reality—has spoken for himself in Jesus Christ. If you want to know who God is, take a look at Jesus—what he *says* and what he *does*. Jesus is not one of the spiritual emanations among the many influences we meet along the way of the spiritual odyssey of our lives. He is the path himself. This is the total claim of the gospel. It is this that makes the gospel so exciting and appealing, and at the same moment it is this totality and radical nature of the gospel that makes it scandalous, an affront to all our religion.

I remember the question-and-answer session that was held at Princeton in 1963 during Karl Barth's Princeton lectures. These lectures were published in Karth Barth, *Evangelical Theology: An Introduction*. One student asked Dr. Barth, "Sir, don't you think God has revealed himself in other religions and not only in Christianity?" Barth's answer was like a shock of bright lightning in that packed lounge. He answered, "No, God has not revealed himself in any religion, including Christianity. He has revealed himself in his Son." That is it! "In Jesus Christ, God has spoken for himself, and we must hear that speech."

The Barmen Declaration of 1934, framed by Confessing Christians in Germany in the midst of their crisis of identity and temptation, gives to us a theological commentary upon this crucial text of John's Gospel. Here is article one.

> 1. "I am the way, and the truth, and the life; no one comes to the Father, but by me" (John 14:6). "Truly, truly, I say to you, he who does not enter the sheepfold by the door but climbs in by another way, that man is a thief and a robber. . . . I am the door; if anyone enters by me, he will be saved." (John 10:1, 9).
>
> Jesus Christ, as he is attested for us in Holy Scripture, is the one Word of God which we have to hear and which we have to trust and obey in life and in death.
>
> We reject the false doctrine, as though the Church could and would have to acknowledge as a source of its proclamation, apart from and besides this one Word of God, still other events and powers, figures and truths, as God's revelation *(Book of Confessions, 808–.19)*.

If we are to argue with the Christian gospel, it is right that we have the true and important place to debate, because here we are at the very center.

In his answer to Philip Jesus continues to assure his friend of the durability of their relationship. Later in this commentary we will examine Jesus' teaching on prayer, but note here that the Lord promises the disciples that they will participate in even greater works than they have already witnessed. I believe *greater* should be seen in its sense of wider, larger. These twelve, and the somewhat larger circle of men and women who have followed Jesus, are in for a surprise beyond their greatest expectations when following Pentecost they will see thousands of men and women, young and old, slave and free, Greek and Jew, come to trust in Jesus Christ as Lord and Savior with the same faith as these disciples now experience. These disciples will share in and enjoy that great and wide expansion of the family of believers.

The Holy Spirit comes from God to make the disciples' relationship to Jesus continuing and real.

29. The Holy Companion
John 14:15-31

"I will pray the Father, and he will give you another Counselor, to be with you for ever." With these words Jesus begins to teach his disciples about the ministry of the Holy Spirit in their lives.

I want now to describe the elements of that teaching so that we may see this portrayal in its totality. The teaching begins with the relationship already present and real. "If you love me, you will keep my commandments." We trust Christ because we love him, and loving and trusting him, we follow him. But that trust relationship has two sides. We trust, but the question that naturally follows is: what does God do? We love him and follow him as disciples; now our Lord will reveal to his disciples the other side of that relationship.

(1) "The Father ... will give." In the New Testament we see the Holy Spirit as coming from the Father and the Son interchangeably. Note verse 18, "I will come to you." There is no confusion in the mind of Jesus. The Father and the Son are one. Now added to that unity is the Holy Spirit who comes from them to us.

(2) "Another *parakletos*." This Greek word means literally, "the one who is called alongside," therefore, a companion, counselor—*para*, along side, *kletos* from the root word meaning "to call." As Jesus had come alongside of his disciples during their journey together, so another companion not different from Jesus Christ but coming from him will journey alongside them. This word is also used by other New Testament writers in their explanation of the ministry of the Holy Spirit. Notice Paul's use of the word in 2 Cor. 1:3-7. As a verb it is also the word used to communicate encouragement in Titus 1:9, and Colossians 4:8, " ... that he may encourage your hearts."

(3) "The Spirit of truth." The word *spirit* in Greek is also the word for *wind*, as it is in Hebrew. The force of the Greek phrase is

that the Spirit brings truth because the Spirit belongs to truth. Jesus here has assured the disciples that the wind from God will not blow the disciples into false pathways.

A criterion for testing the many small winds that come across our lives is also implied in this promise. God's Spirit is bound to and belongs to the truth that he has already shown in Jesus Christ. John will pick up this implication in his first epistle: "Beloved, do not believe every spirit, but test the spirits to see whether they are of God; for many false prophets have gone out into the world. By this you know the Spirit of God: every spirit which confesses that Jesus Christ has come in the flesh is of God" (1 John 4:1-2).

(4)"He dwells with you, and will be in you." Here we have the verb related to the noun "dwelling place" we noted in 14:2. The counselor abides with the disciples and in them. The relationship is very rich indeed.

(5) "I will not leave you desolate." The word translated "desolate" means "like orphans." By this promise Jesus recognizes that the disciples will feel as if they have been left alone in the world, but he contradicts their feelings, and the promise answers their fear. As the Holy Spirit comes to them, it will be Christ who comes: "I will come to you." Jesus affirms his ultimate victory over death in the context of this promise. "Because I live, you will live also." We are identified with the victory of Christ as surely as we are identified with his death. It will be the Holy Spirit who will assure us of that identification.

(6) The other Judas, one of the disciples not otherwise mentioned in John, now asks a very important question that disciples of Christ in every age have also asked: How will this wondrous assurance take place? "Lord, how is it that you will manifest yourself to us and not to the world?" The answer Jesus gives is not complicated by either ritual or religious practices. He says simply that as the disciples love Christ and obey his words, the Father will take on the responsibility for authenticating and assuring them of his love for them. "... my Father will love him, and we will come to him, and make our home with him." The word translated *home* in verse 23 is the very same Greek word used at the opening of the chapter in verse 2: "In my father's house are many *rooms*."

(7) "The Holy Spirit, whom the Father will send in my name, he will teach you all things, and bring to your remembrance all that I have said to you." Here once again the relationship between Christ and the Spirit is preserved. Jesus goes on to say that the Holy Spirit will be the teacher of the disciples in keeping them reminded of what he had done and said. The implication is that the Holy

Spirit does not teach new truth beyond what has been revealed in Christ. He reminds and assures the disciples of the truth already revealed in Christ. The connection between the Holy Spirit and Jesus Christ is inseparable.

(8) "Peace I leave with you." Jesus promises that in him is a health and soundness that is greater than what the world knows; therefore the disciples need not be thrown into confusion when the reality of evil confronts them.

Jesus has drawn together the threads of Holy Spirit teaching that have already appeared in the Gospel: "I saw the Spirit descend as a dove . . ." (1:32); "The wind blows where it wills . . ." (3: 5-8); "God is spirit, and those who worship . . ." (4:24). There are two ways to draw together these teachings that are two sides of the same coin. The Holy Spirit is God himself assuring the believer of Jesus Christ after first convicting us of our thirst (16:8). Therefore, when we are able to trust in Christ and to feel assured in our hearts that he is our Lord, it is the Holy Spirit who has assured us. That assurance is experienced by us because of the confirmation of the Holy Spirit granted to us.

The other great theme in Holy Spirit teaching emphasizes the mystery that within the character of God—in his very essence— there is fellowship. Therefore, Jesus Christ can speak without any artificiality that he loves the Father and that the Father loves him. The Holy Spirit descends as a dove upon Christ as part of their inner relationship of love. God does not exist in splendid isolation; there is love and relationship *within* his very nature—Father, Son, Holy Spirit.

30. *"My Joy in You"*
John 15:1–11

According to John's narrative, Jesus is now walking with his disciples from the place of the last Supper to the garden of Gethsemane. As they walk, he tells a parable similar in some ways to his earlier parable of the sheepfold (John 10). This one is also told in the Jewish form of the mashal.

Their walk that evening would have taken them near the temple. One of its notable features, according to Josephus (*Antiquities,* xv–x1.3), was a golden vine and clusters "as large as a man."

We know from the Feast of Tabernacles discourses that Jesus built his teaching upon the symbols that were already a part of the people's life. This figure of the vine is another one of those instances. There are a large number of Old Testament references to vines and vineyards, trees and branches. (See Jer. 6:9; Ps. 80; Ezek. 15). One very interesting Old Testament image appears in Ezekiel 17 and is portrayed in very personal language. Jesus has taken hold of a common symbol out of the people's history and now uses it to tell a new story.

It is clear, therefore, that the Old Testament background for this image is well established. The thesis of Bultmann (p. 407) that this parable has its source in Gnostic tree-of-life myths as found in the Mandean literature is founded upon a faulty chronology. It is the Mandean literature and Gnostic writers who borrow from both New and Old Testament sources rather than the reverse.

The parable begins with another of the "I am" statements: "I am the true vine and my Father is the vine dresser." In the image of the vine Jesus repeats a theme that he has stated forcefully in the opening of this discourse: "I am the way, the truth and the life." Everything that now follows in this parable has to do with the close relationship between the disciples and Jesus. Jesus will open different possibilities in the image in order to make clear to his disciples what it means that they will *dwell* in the Father and that the

Father and Son by the Holy Spirit will dwell with and in them. We see this parable, therefore, as an explanation of themes introduced in 13:31–14:31. We have already noted that the word *abide* used some ten times in the parable is related to the word *dwelling* that appeared in 14:2. The other themes are also drawn together by this image and Jesus' explanation of it, as we shall see.

Jesus begins the image with a warning that is obvious to any grape grower: "Every branch of mine that bears no fruit, he takes away, and [later] . . . if a man does not abide in me, he is cast forth as a branch and withers; and the branches are gathered, thrown into the fire and burned." We must be careful to notice what Jesus says and also what he does not say in these warnings. The first warning is the simple and matter-of-fact statement that the branches are meant for fruit and that this is their purpose. A little later in the mashal and its interpretation, it will become clearer what Jesus means by his use of the word *fruit*. But for now the warning is that the branches are meant by the Great Vinedresser to bear fruit, unlike a wild vine where each branch may do as it pleases, go where it will and perhaps avoid the grapes altogether if it so desires. This vine is not to be the vine of tiny sour grapes which Middle Easterners found on vineyards gone wild, but this is the true vine with the true grapes. The branches are invited into this vine if they desire to share in its goal.

It is important to keep the *freedom* ingredient in the discipleship teaching of Jesus clear in our minds all of the time that we ponder this mashal. The grape branches we know about in the Napa Valley do not exercise choice as to their connection with the main vine or fruit-bearing. But in this mashal, as in Old Testament images of Israel as a vineyard, the freedom ingredient is essential in order to make sense both of the warning that Jesus gives at the opening and also of the discipleship instruction he gives later in the proverb.

Jesus warns that every branch that does not stay related to the vine will wither. This also is an obvious implication of the image. Jesus is not saying to his disciples that they, in fact, will become fruitless or that they will cease to abide. He is, instead, giving the kind of instruction that a rock-climbing instructor on a perilous mountaineering expedition might give to his student climbers. He will point up the safety procedures that will be used. He will describe the rope, carabiners and pitons that will secure the climbers during each separate negotiation in the climb. He may say something like this: "We have a two-thousand-pound test rope, and it will hold any of you in a fall as we belay you in a safe stop, but you should all realize that there is no other back-up system. If this rope fails you in such a crisis, you will have made a much more speedy descent than we anticipated." This instructor is not expecting his climbers to break the nylon rope, but he must impress upon them its importance to them and the plain fact that if it should fail in a fall, though it won't, there is no other hope for the climber.

Jesus invites his disciples to decide how they stand with the vine. If the branches were to break away from the vine, then there is no other vine that will give them life, just as there is no other back-up secret rope or stairway for the mountaineer. Jesus does not imply or say that these disciples will break away, but it would not fit in with the realism and honesty of Jesus as a teacher were he not to make it clear to his disciples that the purpose of this vine is fruit. And that is not bad news but good news. He tells them plainly that the branch must be related, must abide, in the true source—there is no other source able to sustain the vine. That also is not bad news but good news. If the mountaineer chooses to trust the rope, the rope has more than enough strength to stand by him or her. This is not bad news but good news.

It is my view that this is the logic employed in an important passage in the Book of Hebrews (6:1–8). That writer creates the same hypothetical argument: suppose a Christian were dissatisfied with the redemption there is in Christ and were anxious to move on to perhaps some greater height or better source for life; the argument might run as follows, "Jesus was a good starting point, but now I must move on to greater spiritual heights." The writer to the Hebrews warns such a person that there is no other source for salvation and life but what we have in Christ. If we were to break the rope, we must remember that there is no other one. He has not taught that the rope will break. Instead he insists that there is simply no other rope.

Now we come to a fuller interpretation of the image. Jesus tells us that when a branch dwells in relationship with the vine, the Father will *clean out* the branch. The RSV translates the Greek word *katharizo* as *prune*. The English word *cathartic* comes from this Greek root. The point is, Jesus tells us, that the branch is worked with and disciplined, trimmed and cleaned by the Father so that it may bear fruit and fulfill its destiny.

"You are already made clean by the word which I have spoken to you." There is a play on Greek words here. The adjective translated "clean" is the Greek word *katharos*. It is significant for us to notice in this image what exactly it is that the branch is urged to concentrate upon. The branch does not prune or "cleanse" itself—

God does that for the branch. The branch has one major choice and that choice is to abide in the vine. It has a secondary choice and that is to bear fruit. The fruit is the natural result of a healthy relationship with the vine and the pruning. In terms of the freedom elements present in the mashal, the branch also plays a key role in the fruit, as Jesus' telling of the image makes clear. But first things first. The fruit comes after and as a consequence of the abiding relationship. *Abide* then becomes the most crucial link to our understanding of what Christian faith means. That word shows that, at the very heart of it all, *faith* is primarily a relationship word.

"If you abide in me . . . ask whatever you will. . . . " The freedom ingredient in the image is now heightened. The branch is to ask for help in order "that you bear much fruit . . . " (vv. 7, 8).

"Abide in my love." The relationship of branch and vine is not mechanical or agricultural. It is a personal relationship. In Christian faith we do not attach ourselves to a great truth-force or status of things, nor do we search within our own inner selves for divine principles. The Christian by faith abides in Jesus Christ, knows and experiences and enjoys his love. Jesus concludes this part of the image with the promise of joy to those who abide in the vine and who are disciples of the vine.

The Greek word *chara*, "joy," is related to the word *charis*, "grace." It has about it a sense of surprise and excitement. Jesus is teaching us that the result of our obedience to his will for life results in the exciting and liberating experience of his love—"that your joy may be full" (v. 11). Joy is the virtue continuously promised to us by the world, but in reality it is "the gigantic secret of the Christian" (G. K. Chesterton, *Orthodoxy*, p. 160). This surprising joy Jesus now promises to his disciples. This joy, and all of the love, freedom, sacrifice, hard work, relationship, purpose, and integrity that go with it, is the fruit that the branches are privileged to bear. The fruit of the branches is not more branches (souls won) but fruit—the good results of being with Jesus Christ. Indeed, those good results do win others.

Athletes and sportsmen know from experience that the greatest enjoyment of any sports event comes to those who obey the principles and rules essential to the event—whether it is the fault line in tennis or the principles of rope belay in rock climbing. Every game withers when an athlete or team ignores the truth of the event. Jesus teaches his disciples that they will enjoy their discipleship in proportion to their obedience—their willingness to really trust in and live out the liberating truth of the gospel.

*The kind of love Jesus commands
his disciples to have for one another
will affect the world positively and
negatively.*

31. *"You Are My Friends"*
John 15:12-27

Jesus continues to explain the parable of the vine and branches by further interpreting the intimate meaning of the relationship between vine and branches.

He begins by repeating the sentence that he had spoken earlier in the evening (see 13:34). "This is my commandment that you love one another as I have loved you." This is the new commandment. We are expected by Jesus to love not only because he commands it but also because he loves us. Our love of one another and of the world—the setting of this passage is placed by Jesus into a world context by the next paragraph—is a result of our being first loved.

Now we must ask a vital question: What does this word *love—agapē* (noun, *agapaō* verb) mean? Our search of the Greek lexicon is very little help to us in understanding the word. Classical Greek uses *agapē* only sparingly. In classical usage it is a bland, colorless word which means "good will" and is used without any special significance. (See the discussion in Earl Palmer, *Love Has Its Reasons*, pp. 51-52.) The noun *agapē* first gains its New Testament meaning by its use in the Septuagint (the Greek translation of the Old Testament written about 100 B.C.). It is the rich Hebrew love vocabulary of the Old Testament which wins the day, and we see this simple little word *agapē* used to translate the active and faithful love of the God of Abraham, Isaac and Jacob; it is therefore through our observance of its use that we discover its meaning.

But in an even more profound way, we discover what love means by watching what Jesus does. "In this is love, not that we loved God but that he loved us and sent his Son . . ." (1 John 4:10). Love is an event more than a word. "Greater love has no man than this, that a man lay down his life for his friends." It is this love that identifies with the disciples to the uttermost and that will become the enabling within them to make their love a possibility. In the opening part of the image of the vine Jesus emphasized the disciples' abiding in the vine; now Jesus affirms the mystery of how the vine will abide in the branch. Love holds on; Jesus will hold on to his disciples even into the terrible valley of their death itself, and at the moment when they are to perish he will take their place. That is love.

But Jesus draws out a further conclusion. He shows the effect that love has in relationships. Love creates friendship and the sharing in goals and purposes. *Philoi* is the word translated *friends*. The related verb *phileō* is used in John's Gospel sometimes as a synonym for *agapaō*, though John usually favors *agapaō* in his treatment of the love of God. *Phileō* expresses the love that is natural and instinctive as, for example, the love a person feels toward wisdom—hence, *philosophy*—or toward a brother—hence, *philadelphia*—or toward mankind in general—hence, *philanthrophy*. It implies in its ordinary usage an intimacy of shared purpose or blood relationship. Jesus teaches here that the result of agape love at work in his disciples is the development of just this sort of shared goals and relationships; it is the beautiful intimacy between people who trust each other.

J. R. R. Tolkien has captured something of this aspect of love in the insistence of Sam Gamgi who will not allow his master Frodo to travel alone to meet the dreadful dangers ahead across the plains of Mordor. His love for Frodo has made him a friend—the old servant-master relationship is altered as Sam, with wide open eyes, enters upon the mission of Frodo to defeat the power of the ring. Together in this friendship now, they are united in the same purpose. They are friends. It is agape that did this (J. R. R. Tolkien, *The Fellowship of the Ring*, p. 422).

We are grateful for our Lord's teaching on love. Very often agape love is interpreted so completely as an act of our will in obedience to the command of Christ that we lose the sense of this warm and shared relationship which Jesus makes so essential to the total portrayal.

Jesus concludes his interpretation of the figure of the vine and branches by reminding his disciples that it is he who first chose them. He puts this divine choice into dialectic tension with the choices that the disciple makes. It would be theologically and biblically incorrect to diminish either side of this dialectical tension. Christ chooses and yet he preserves our freedom to choose. We choose and yet it is Christ who first chose us.

It would be a misunderstanding of the total witness of the texts to teach either that: (1) Christ's choice overwhelms our choice, or (2) our choice is made completely by ourselves apart from his grace which first found us. The first option fails to recognize that our freedom is part of God's sovereign decision. The second option fails to recognize that "we love because he first loved us."

The next paragraph relates to the previous section in the fact that Jesus makes clear to his disciples that they will share in his ministry within a less than ideal setting, that is to say, within the real world. They are not to be surprised by the hatred of the world. Their friendship with Christ does not mean that the world will honor that friendship. The fact is that as the world resents Christ so he prepares his disciples in a very matter-of-fact way not to be surprised by their own experiences of a similar resentment.

Nevertheless, Jesus tells his disciples that they are to be his witnesses in that very world. There their love will face severe new tests, but it will also make its impact felt. Jesus here begins a theme which will become a major focus in chapters 16, 17, 20 and 21; the mission task of the disciples is to be witnesses to Christ in the world.

The disciples are "not of the world." Jesus means by that the fact that we Christians derive the meaning for our existence, our worth, and our task from the decision God made about us and not out of our existence itself, or the world as the immediate context of our existence. This does not result in an escapist attitude toward the world, as we shall see in the next chapters but, in fact, in a more profoundly helpful relationship toward the whole created order.

32. The Witness to Justice
John 16:1-15

This final chapter in Jesus' Thursday eve discourse begins on the very bleak prediction about the world situation that his disciples may expect to find. We need not seek for understanding of these hard words in speculations about the nature of early church trials and experiences of rejection now justified after the fact by the introduction of these words (John 16:1-3) into John's text. The text stands logically within the teaching context of this material. As Jesus is now rejected by leaders of the Sanhedrin, he predicts the same experience for his followers. The really tragic ingredient in their persecution is that their persecutors will think that they honor God in persecution—"whoever kills you will think he is offering service to God." This is the raw material of tragedy. Jesus is aware of the terrible twists that occur in the lives of men and women, so that often the cruelest of acts are sometimes committed in the very name of God. Jesus announces to his disciples that these people do not know the Father nor the Lord.

One question that will certainly come up among the followers of Jesus in later generations is this: What guidance will Jesus give to us when social and political power has shifted and we who are the disciples of Jesus have such power? Whereas in the first century the Christians are a minority even among the larger Jewish community, what of the situation of a few centuries later when the disciples of Jesus will have won in the contest of ideas, the old Roman Empire will have become the Holy Roman Empire, and the sword of the State will then serve the church? Has Jesus given guidance to us for such a change in political-social status?

He has by the pattern of his own life. Though he had power, he did not use it against his foes. When he had public support, as on Palm Sunday and after the feeding of the multitudes, he did not exploit that real power over the people in a way that would in any

136

way diminish the freedom of the people to choose against him.

Now in this remarkable passage Jesus gives to his disciples a theological perspective by which to answer the question. He again assures the disciples that he will send the Holy Companion: "and when he comes, he will convince the world of sin and of righteousness and of judgment." The Greek word translated "convince" is the word *elenchein* which was earlier used in 8:46 when Jesus asked his accusors, "Which of you *convicts* me of sin?" This word may be translated "bring to light, expose, set forth, convict, convince." As a noun it is the word *proof*, as in Hebrews 11:1, "proving of things unseen . . ." Paul uses this word in Ephesians 5:11: "take no part in unfruitful works of darkness, but instead *expose* them." It is used in the book of Revelation (3:19): "Those whom I love I *reprove* . . ." John uses the word early in this Gospel: "for every one who does evil hates the light, and does not come to the light, lest his deeds should be *exposed*" (3:30). From these examples we can better understand this interesting Greek word. (As you can see from these quotations, translators use different English words to translate the same Greek word, which is why we must read back behind the English text to how the word was used when the New Testament documents were first written—therefore the need for Greek word studies.)

When Jesus says about the Holy Spirit that "when he comes, he will convince the world of sin and of righteousness and of judgment" using the word *elenchein*, he has taken out of the hands of his disciples the rod of punishment against those who reject Jesus Christ as Lord. We do not have the obligation of proving to our neighbors the fact that they are sinners. That is the task of the Holy Spirit. He is the one who will expose creatively the hurts and empty places of the world.

The task of the disciples of Jesus Christ is to know the truth. "When the spirit of truth comes, he will guide you into all the truth." It is also to affirm to the world the truth with its implications. It will be the responsibility of God to authenticate our witness and to break through the barriers of hardness toward Christ. Notice that Jesus does not use destructive language with regard to the world in its sin. He uses confrontation language. The Holy Spirit exposes and brings into focus—creativity opens up the emptiness of sin so that the world may be able to see. Even in this choice of words, we recognize Jesus' decision to preserve the freedom of men and women to discover and see. These sinners are not shattered and overwhelmed by the work of the Holy Spirit. They are confronted with reality. Even this is not bad news. It is good news. Though it is the salty side of the gospel, nevertheless it is good to know the truth. Therefore the prophetic task of the Christian in the world is primarily the positive task of affirmation of the truth and daring to spell out its implications into the personal and social realities of life.

The Lion, the Witch, and the Wardrobe is C. S. Lewis's first novel in the Chronicles of Narnia. When the four British children are told that they were brought to Narnia to meet Aslan, the son of the Emperor beyond the Sea, they are at first delighted at the honor. (Aslan is the Christ figure throughout the Chronicles.) But then in further discussion it comes out that Aslan is a great lion. Now they are not so sure they are up to meeting him. Lucy is uneasy and nervous. "Is he quite safe?" she asks one of the family of talking beavers they are staying with. Mr. Beaver answers, "Safe? . . . 'Course he isn't safe. But he's good" (p. 64).

Jesus has already created a great uneasiness by his ministry. He has shown the world its sins. He is not safe; he is the Lord and he exposes who we are. He threatens the status quo. What is very important for us to see is that this *exposing* is in our favor and the world's favor. It is God who does the exposing. I am not so sure it would be good news if we Christians were to be charged with such a task. Not that we don't enjoy the right of judgment, but that is exactly the problem! We enjoy judgment too much. It has a cumulative power over us and tends to break our solidarity with the people around us. We see ourselves as set over against the neighbor. Jesus gives to us a greater power than the power of judgment, and that is the gift of his life. "He who abides in me, and I in him, he it is that bears much fruit." "You did not choose me, but I chose you and appointed you that you should go and bear fruit and that your fruit should abide."

Therefore, the disciples are to have a positive, affirmative task in the world, and God himself will prepare the way. Jesus Christ, who by the act of his sovereign grace convicted a mob of their own sins in the dangerous scene of the woman caught in adultery, has here promised the same convicting sovereign grace in his promise of the ministry of the Holy Spirit in the world.

33. The Disciples and the World
John 16:16–33

Jesus draws his last discourse to its close with a reminder of words he spoke at the beginning of the discourse: "A little while, and you will see me no more.... The hour is coming ... when you will be scattered, every man to his home, and will leave me alone" (vv. 16, 32). Jesus' speech begins and ends with his realism. He knows his disciples, and their weakness is no shock to him.

This realism is a very important ingredient in the gospel. It shows not only the fraility of the Christian but that Jesus Christ has taken into account that fraility. In the Acts and the Epistles, we discover that this fraility is still applicable, even following the resurrection of Jesus Christ and the confirmation of his victory by the Holy Spirit at Pentecost. The Holy Spirit will assure our hearts of Christ's victory but he will not take away our freedom, our real choices. Therefore Jesus' realism about the disciples who are walking with him to Gethsemane is important and helpful for us in the twentieth century. Like those first-century disciples, we will need the help of Jesus Christ to make it and to survive in our generation.

Jesus does not predict that the disciples will collapse into endless self-recrimination and regret because of their weakness at the coming time of trial. That kind of despair language is not present at all in this discourse. Despair is regret that can see no possible way beyond itself. Jesus shares with his disciples a parable that they are unable to understand but that will later become clear to them. "When a woman is in travail ... " He interprets the image as follows: "You will be sorrowful, but your sorrow will turn into joy.... So you have sorrow now, but I will see you again and your hearts will rejoice" (vv. 21, 20, 22). The profound grief that results from the failures of the disciples is not the last word. The promise stands: they will share in Christ's victory and then their questions will be resolved.

But the disciples will need help to work it all through and to discover the joy beyond the sorrow. It is in this context that Jesus teaches his disciples about prayer. This teaching begins with the middle of verse 23: "Amen, amen, I say to you, if you ask anything of the Father, he will give it to you in my name." In this teaching, the usual Greek word for prayer is not used by Jesus. The RSV text reads for verse 26, "I shall pray the Father for you," but actually "pray" translates the Greek word *erotan,* which means "to ask." That same word was used in verses 23a and 30.

A synonym for *erotan* is used in 23b, *aitein* which also means "to ask." By these simple, down-to-earth words—not heavy religious words, like the Greek *evoke* (pray), which in classical Greek implies the idea of vow, bargain—Jesus teaches his disciples simply to bring their whole selves, who they are and what they feel, to the Father. "There are no limits to what we may pray" (Helmut Thielicke). Jesus encourages his disciples to come simply and directly with the questions that are on our hearts. He promises that "the Father will give it to you in my name." Somehow in prayer we are given an authority—"ask anything"—yet at the same time the authority of Jesus Christ is preserved—"in my name." Here again Jesus gives us a teaching that is dialectical. He has posed a tension between our authority on the one side, our privilege in asking, and on the other side his authority and reign over us. This tension is never compromised throughout the New Testament when prayer is endorsed for the church and experienced among the Christians.

The words of Jesus on prayer have been encouraging teaching which the disciples understand. "Ah, now you are speaking plainly, not in any figure!" (v. 29). The word here translated "figure" is the Greek word *paroimia* which is the translation of the Hebrew *mashal* in the Septuagint. As we observed earlier, it is used as a synonym for *parabole,* parable. The disciples express their faith in Jesus Christ as their Lord.

The final words of Jesus become a pastoral summation of the discourse: "I have said this to you, that in me you may have peace. In the world you have tribulation; but be of good cheer, I have overcome the world." The word translated here as "tribulation" is the word *thlipsis* which was used earlier in this chapter by Jesus in his parable about the woman in travail: "but when she is delivered of the child, she no longer remembers the *anguish.*"

The suffering of the woman in travail is real and awesome, but it is not forever. It is not her last experience or memory. By this choice of the same words we are shown that the tribulation the disciples know in the world is real but not the last word. It is surrounded by a greater reality.

We now are able to draw together the world view as taught by Jesus in this Gospel. A line drawing model may be helpful in explaining the view of history.

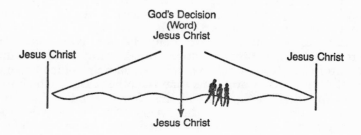

In the Gospel of John we have learned of God's prior existence and his decision/speech who is Jesus Christ—with the Father in the beginning before creation and by whom the creation takes place. In the model, therefore, we have a view of history which sees the order of reality we call heaven and earth created by the decision of God. Therefore Jesus Christ stands before the beginning of history.

I have portrayed the historical existence of the world with a wavy line to symbolize the turbulence caused by our sin, that is, by our bad choices against the will of God. A cosmic line would show the same turbulence because of personal moral will against the will of God at the spiritual realm, which is the devil. At the center is the downward line which radically intersects the wavy line of history. That downward line is Jesus Christ the Word become flesh, alongside of us and in our midst as Savior and Lord. The disciples and all who follow after them live on this side of that great center line. They have a continuity with the wavy line of history before them and ahead of them. In this we see the insistence in the Gospels and all of the New Testament that the disciples in their redemption are not lifted above history and its tribulation by a spiritual escape from the world. The Gnostics yearned for this and taught this "hope," but not the New Testament and certainly not

John. "Redemption" for Gnosticism means escape from the world. Redemption in John means forgiveness and restored relationship with God here and now.

The wavy line continues after the coming, death and victory of Christ because, as we noted earlier, God's decision has not destroyed our freedom. The wavy line goes right through the church, a fact of which the New Testament is proof. "The New Testament letters are not written apart from the problems of the churches" (Barth, *Dogmatics in Outline*, p. 142). We may not like it, and certainly the presence of that turbulent line has been a great offense to Christians throughout the ages. We have even from time to time attempted to deny the fact. Every day, somewhere, another group of Christians breaks away from a nominal and sinful church to establish a "perfect church" which has no, or at least fewer, sins or problems than the others. But such churches are not founded on the basis of the New Testament but on the basis of idealistic visions and the "wish dream" of the group itself. (See Dietrich Bonhoeffer's argument in this regard in *Life Together*, pp. 26–30).

The wavy line represents the turbulence of the world we are to live in, and it is in this real world that we carry out our great task. This means that as Christians we must live out our discipleship in a less than ideal setting. Jesus had predicted it in a famous parable: "Let both [the wheat and the weeds] grow together" (Matt. 13: 30).

But this turbulent line is itself not ultimate, and in that fact we see the third line of the model. Jesus Christ who stands at the beginning of history and at its center also is the one who stands at its fulfillment. History does not end with a whimper of emptiness; the same Jesus Christ stands at its end as he stands at its beginning and its center. "I have overcome the world." This is the victory, as this Gospel narrative will make clear—not against the world but for it. (This same word is used in the same redemptive sense in Rev. 5:5 and 1 Cor. 15:57.)

It is the Holy Spirit who enables the disciples to make it and to carry out their task here and now in this age. The Holy Spirit is God making his decision real to each of us in the midst of the turbulent world.

34. *Prayer for the Disciples*
John 17:1–26

At the close of the farewell address of Moses, we have recorded for us in Deuteronomy 32 a great prayer which is called the Song of Moses. According to John's Gospel, our Lord concludes his last discourse with his disciples with a prayer that could also be called a song or hymn. It is the fulfillment of the Song of Moses. The vindication of *Yahweh* in the prayer of Jesus is spoken of as now complete. The hour of that vindication is here.

This prayer draws together many of the themes that are present in the last discourse teaching and also themes that we find in the prayer Jesus taught his disciples as recorded in the other Gospels. That brief prayer, the "Our Father" (Matt. 6:7–13), opens with the recognition of the glory and reign of God. This prayer of Jesus in John 17 also begins with the recognition of God's glory now revealed in the Son. The "Our Father" prayer prays for the kingly reign of God upon the earth. This prayer asks for holy strength for the disciples to live out the reign of God on the earth. The "Our Father" asks for forgiveness; here Jesus claims for his disciples the wholeness that comes in forgiveness: "Sanctify them in the truth." The "Our Father" asks for strength to forgive others; in this prayer Jesus asks that his love may be in them. The "Our Father" asks for protection against the evil one; in this prayer the same words appear: "that thou shouldst keep them from the evil one."

Jesus begins this prayer, "Father, the hour has come; glorify thy Son." The dramatic phrase "the hour" or "my hour" has been used throughout John's Gospel in a decisive way. By this phrase we discover that God's mighty will is fulfilled in a particular event, a moment, an hour. God's love, therefore, is not a general truth or principle but the love that cares concretely about real people in real places. God's mighty will is God's mighty act, and that act happened in human history. This concreteness does not diminish the

143

timeless eternal meaning of that hour. All of heaven and earth from the beginning to the end of time looks to that hour in awe. From this great prayer we discover that Christ is glorified not only in the resurrection but also by his humiliation at Calvary. It is in the Jesus who dies and is victorious over death that we see the presence of God breaking through to us. The glory of God is more than the show of greatness and magnificence. It is the show of humiliation and lowliness. It is the Jesus with the towel and basin of water as well as the Jesus who conquers the blindness of the young man on the temple steps. Therefore, Jesus' prayer asks that God the Father will show himself, his character, in the whole sequence of events that now will take place. We are so conditioned to think of glory in triumphal terms that we often miss the point of the prayer. This is a prayer on the eve of the total servanthood of Jesus Christ. In that amazing grace of Jesus Christ, the servant Lord, we will see the glory of God! How strong he is to be able to reach so far down! How sure of himself to take even upon himself our death.

C. S. Lewis has caught this New Testament meaning of glory in a parable he tells in his apologetic book *Miracles* (p. 135).

> One has the picture of a strong man stooping lower and lower to get himself underneath some great complicated burden. He must stoop in order to lift, he must almost disappear under the load before he incredibly straightens his back and marches off with the whole mass swaying on his shoulders. Or one may think of a diver, first reducing himself to nakedness, then glancing in mid-air, then gone with a splash, vanished, rushing down through green and warm water into black and cold water, down through increasing pressure into the death-like region of ooze and slime and old decay; then up again, back to colour and light, his lungs almost bursting, till suddenly he breaks surface again, holding in his hand the dripping, precious thing that he went down to recover. He and it are both coloured now that they have come up into the light: down below, where it lay colourless in the dark, he lost his colour too.

He lost his color too! We must create a new definition of glory. Glory is the love of God redeeming the world.

In the second paragraph of the prayer, Jesus prays for his disciples, setting them apart from the world. Yet Jesus prophetically claims that the glory of God will be expressed in the world through these disciples.

One disciple was lost as the scripture had predicted. "I have guarded them, and none of them is lost but the son of perdition,

that the scripture might be fulfilled." Some interpreters feel that
the phrase, "that the scripture might be fulfilled," is John's edito-
rial addition. It is not possible contextually to show this one way or
the other. What scripture does Jesus refer to here? The best clue
from John's Gospel comes in 13:18 where John cites Psalm 41:9 in
connection with Judas: "Even my bosom friend in whom I trusted,
who ate of my bread, has lifted his heel against me." The word
translated "perdition" comes from the root word meaning "perish." In his betrayal of Jesus, Judas has chosen the way of death.
This brief sentence becomes a remarkable psychological reflection
upon the tragedy of betrayal. Whatever may be the temptations
that induce us to go against truth, against people who have trusted
us as friends, that choice to betray is the choice that leads toward
death—both theirs and ours.

The world view that Jesus has taught (in chapter 16) is affirmed
again in verse 15: "I do not pray that thou shouldst take them out
of the world." It is in the turbulent world that the disciples must
live, but we do not receive our meaning from the wavy line—from
history. We receive the meaning of our existence from the decision
God made. Therefore, we are "not of this world." We are to survive
in the world and, by the grace of God, not only to survive but to
fulfill the holy task granted to us. This is because the source of our
worth comes from the decision God made by which he first created
us, by which he redeems us, by which he sustains us, by which he
fulfills us.

"I do not pray for these only." We must observe again that
though the RSV makes use of the English word *pray* throughout
this chapter, the more precise word should be *ask*. It is that simple
word *erotan* that is used.

Jesus now asks in behalf of disciples who will believe in the future. He prays for our oneness: "that they may be one." This
means that the solidarity of the disciples is not just the Apostle
Paul's concern (1 Cor 12); Jesus said it first.

The oneness that the disciples of Jesus Christ experience with
each other is the result of Jesus. E. Stanley Jones expressed the
point of this final part of Jesus' prayer very well in his three-part
sentence: "You belong to Christ; I belong to Christ; we belong to
each other." Jesus is describing the oneness that results from a
shared experience of the presence of God (glory) in the lives of his
people in the world. Jesus prophetically looks to the future and
claims that as the disciples express that solidarity toward each
other in the world, then the world will believe in him.

The mission of the Christian in the world is here given its first theological explanation in the Gospel. The Christian strategy is not portrayed in terms of rugged individualism. There are no apostolic heroes who will be so brave and so strong that they will be able to go it alone in the world. As they supremely need Jesus Christ, they will also need each other. As Christ gives to them the gift of the Holy Spirit to abide in them and with them on the journey, so now he gives them each other. This means that the strategy in the world is to be a people—a holy colony—real people in a real place, set in the midst of the wavy line of history. This colony of men and women will experience and know the Word become flesh —"and these *know* that thou hast sent me." This word *know* is not used in the Gnostic sense of the perception of mysteries but in the more earthy Hebrew sense of to know personally and intimately by experience. This means that as Christians together experience the reality of the love of Christ in the real situations of life and as they share that creative love with those around them by this modeling of the love of Christ, then the world is drawn to consider the meaning of God's love.

In this prayer Jesus has given a very important clue concerning the nature of the Christian church, which we need to reflect upon. Jesus creates the oneness which is the church (the gathering of disciples). The basis for the solidarity of the believers is the Lord who makes us one. Christians have often tried to build oneness on the basis of other great facts, but such a basis for solidarity is false.

For example, the mission of the church is not the basis for our solidarity. It is our task but not our motivation. Too much task orientation in the church and the result is that the believers relate to each other on the basis of the giftedness of each believer, and gradually the worth of the brother/sister is shifted to false ground. The basis of our relating is Christ in us. His love is the source of the oneness and from him we derive the task.

The mutual interests of the disciples are not the motivational source for the oneness that Jesus is praying for, whatever those reasons for mutuality are, whether racial likeness, national origins, political agreement, etc. Mutuality is the key to the oneness of the tennis club or the trade union but not Christians. We are brought together because of Christ's invitation, and the people he puts us alongside of may well be "that very selection of neighbors we have been avoiding all week" (C. S. Lewis, *The Screwtape Letters*, p. 12).

The only criteria that Jesus makes mention of are his sovereign decision and our faith. Christ is the one who invites, and whoever believes knows that he or she has been invited because the love that our faith responds to is prior to our faith.

The prayer ends with an affirmation—"I made known to them thy name, and I will make it known, that the love with which thou hast loved me may be in them, and I in them."

Now we know the holy strategy of God in the world—these eleven disciples and those who will also follow Christ, placed in the real world and granted only one tactic, to live out the love of Jesus Christ together.

Now we are to discover the full meaning of that costly love.

35. The Night
John 18:1-11

The four Gospel writers are in agreement concerning the main events of the death and resurrection of Jesus, though they differ in details at certain points, and each writer has certain elements in the narrative which are not present in the others. New Testament scholars believe that the first written form of the Christian message may well have been accounts of the trial, death and resurrection of Jesus Christ which, they hypothesize, are incorporated into the Gospel accounts. Luke tells us that, in fact, he has made use of earlier writings in composing his Gospel: "It seemed good to me also ... to write an orderly account" (1:1). Notice his word *also*. He has followed closely what has been said, and we presume he means what has been written as well.

When we come to John's account, once again there is evidence that John is aware of the other Gospel writers and perhaps even other very early written sources that have been lost to us. But at the same time John has his own knowledge of the events. I believe that the case for the apostolic authorship of this book becomes most compelling in these final chapters. There is an abundant amount of very precise detail and small points that are signs of a book written by one actually present at the event. Once again John's style is not simply to repeat narrative features that by his time of writing are already circulating in the churches as written Gospels: Mark, Matthew and perhaps also Luke. There are essential points that naturally will be told again, but as we have observed, throughout his book John writes a more intensive and interior account, and therefore he notes fewer elements, though each of these elements receives more attention.

The events of the crucifixion begin in a garden across the Kidron valley. Mark and Matthew name the place as Gethsemane. Luke simply locates it on the Mount of Olives.

Each Gospel records the swift-moving events of the betrayal and arrest with different bits of dialogue. These differences between the accounts are very important as historical markers of the integrity of the event. They show by their differences that the event is actual and swift and that the witnesses each report pieces and parts of the whole that were most impressive to them. It is precisely the fact of these divergences that, from a historical point of reference, builds our confidence in the trustworthiness of the event itself. Any trial lawyer who has taken depositions from witnesses knows the importance of these small differences.

As an example of this, notice in this one moment of betrayal and arrest the differences between the New Testament writers as to the dialogue. Matthew tells of the kiss by Judas (Matt. 26:49–50): "And he came up to Jesus at once and said, 'Hail Master!' And he kissed him. Jesus said to him, 'Friend, why are you here?' " After describing the arrest and Peter's attack upon the servant of the high priest, Matthew continues (26:52–54):

> Then Jesus said to [Peter],"Put your sword back into its place; for all who take the sword will perish by the sword. Do you think that I cannot appeal to my Father, and he will at once send me more than twelve legions of angels? But how then should the scriptures be fulfilled, that it must be so?"

In Mark (14:45–52) the account is told as follows: Judas comes up to Jesus having said that a kiss would be the sign.

> And when he came, he went up to him at once, and said, "Master!" And he kissed him. And they laid hands on him and seized him. But one of those who stood by drew his sword, and struck the slave of the high priest and cut off his ear. And Jesus said to them, "Have you come out as against a robber, with swords and clubs to capture me? Day after day I was with you in the temple teaching, and you did not seize me. But let the scriptures be fulfilled." And they all forsook him and fled.
>
> And a young man followed him, with nothing but a linen cloth about his body; and they seized him, but he left the linen cloth and ran away naked.

Mark writes in a clipped, high action style. He alone includes the detail of the naked runner. (Is this an autograph of Mark?)

Luke's account (23:47–53) is again different in detail from Matthew and Mark:

While he was still speaking, there came a crowd, and the man called Judas, one of the twelve, was leading them. He drew near to Jesus to kiss him; but Jesus said to him, "Judas would you betray the Son of man with a kiss?" And when those who were about him saw what would follow, they said, "Lord shall we strike with the sword?" And one of them struck the slave of the high priest and cut off his right ear. But Jesus said, "No more of this!" And he touched his ear and healed him. Then Jesus said to the chief priests and officers of the temple and elders, who had come out against him, "Have you come out as against a robber, with swords and clubs? When I was with you day after day in the temple, you did not lay hands on me. But this is your hour, and the power of darkness."

As we can see, each account is different, very much as three separate wire services—UPI, Reuters, Japan News Service—all reporting on the same public news event, will each send a somewhat different story to different national news services for the next day's papers in New York, London and Tokyo.

Now we come to the Gospel of John. John agrees in essential detail with the other accounts. Judas is accompanied by soldiers and officers from the chief priests and Pharisees. But we also see the more interior nature of John. "Jesus, knowing all that was to befall him . . ." This is the characteristic kind of statement we have come to expect from John. As I have stated earlier, such a sentence as this is permissible if the document were written either long after the event and all close witnesses have died or by someone very close to the person, so close that he knows the inner feelings and assessment of the immediate situation. John, the disciple, has already narrated for us Jesus' final discourse in which the Lord has prepared his disciples for this hour and therefore John is able realistically to make the statement, "Jesus knowing all that was to befall him."

John tells us that Jesus said, " 'Whom do you seek?' They answered him, 'Jesus of Nazareth.' Jesus said to them, 'I am he.' " This great phrase that John has noted so often in his Gospel now comes again in its starkest and most singular sense—"I am," *ego eimi*. We feel the same awe that Moses must have felt at the bush near Mt. Sinai when God made himself known—"I am who I am."

John chooses not to repeat a narrative of the act of betrayal by Judas but instead to record some of the dialogue that is not reported in the other Gospels. He also tells of Peter's attempt to defend Jesus and adds another detail characteristic of someone who notices the names of people: he tells the name of the slave, *Mal-*

chus. It is Luke the physician who records the miracle of healing that Jesus did for this slave. John tells us the slave's name. Relatives of this slave will play a part in events to follow concerning Peter.

The temple guards have come to arrest Jesus with the approval of the Pharisees. Jesus accepts this arrest. Each Gospel makes that fact clear, and John adds the comment concerning Jesus' inner feelings. Jesus rejects the sword of Peter as a defense of his honor. He will take care of his own honor.

Peter's act is an act of panic—a sudden flash of impulsive desperation. Throughout the history of Christendom, when Christians have reached for the sword to defend the honor of Christ, the result has dishonored the gospel. Peter's act is the response of moral fanaticism to a dangerous situation. "The fanatic thinks that his single-minded principles qualify him to do battle with the powers of evil; but like a bull he rushes at the red cloak instead of at the person who is holding it; he exhausts himself and is beaten. He gets entangled in non-essentials and falls into the trap set by cleverer people" (Dietrich Bonhoeffer, *Letters and Papers from Prison*, p. 4).

But there is a deeper theological reality present here. Jesus and he alone is to be the world's Savior. The disciples are not able nor are they permitted by Jesus to intervene. Their moral courage and their moral purity is no match for the power of sin and death. It is this note that each Gospel makes clear in different ways as they all recount the swift-moving events of the arrest in the garden.

Jesus has shown to history a new authority and power. He neither evades his captors nor destroys their meager authority of swords and lanterns and accusers. Jesus Christ will prove his kingship in the very midst of the Thursday-Friday intrigues that have snared him.

36. A Trial
John 18:12–40

"First they led him to Annas, for he was the father-in-law of
Caiaphas." This is a detail only told by John, and later in the account he refers to Annas as high priest. John does not mean that
there are two high priests, since he has already shown his awareness that Caiaphas is the high priest (11:45–53). Annas had been
high priest A.D. 6 to 15. He was a very wealthy man at the time of
his removal from office by Valerius Gratus, and eventually through
the wit and skill of this crafty old man, his five sons and his son-in-
law Caiaphas were all to become high priests.

The most successful of these was Caiaphas, who was high priest
from A.D. 18 to 36. Caiaphas evidently had a close working relationship with the Roman representative at Jerusalem, the procurator
Pilate; in fact when Pilate is deposed, Caiaphas falls from power at
the same time. Therefore, though Caiaphas is technically the high
priest, John shrewdly recognizes that Annas still holds significant
power behind the scenes. John calls him high priest, not out of ig-
norance, as some interpreters have suggested, but for precisely the
opposite reason. It is because John is very well versed on the real
power formation at the time of the trial that he gives us this evidence about Annas and continues to honor him with the title.
Some critics have recently speculated that many highly orthodox
Jews would still have continued to refer to Annas as high priest,
(see F. F. Bruce, *New Testament History*, p. 61; also R. E. Brown,
Gospel According to John, p. 820) in expression of their outrage at
the fact that Roman government had deposed Annas. The Old
Testament (Num. 35:25) states that the office of high priest was
for life and therefore not to be vacated and filled at the pleasure of
Roman authority.

John tells that Peter follows Jesus to this place of interrogation.
He also mentions "another disciple" who was known to the high

152

priest and was able to gain entrance into the courtyard of the palace of Annas. We conclude that this other disciple is our writer. We know John's family is wealthy and certainly his mother is ambitious for her sons. It is not unreasonable to assume that the family of Zebedee may have influential contacts in Jerusalem.

Each Gospel tells of the denials of Peter, and John adds additional information; it is a relative of Malchus who asks the third question of Peter. Peter's answers are not as extreme in John's narrative as in the other Gospels; John reports only the facts in a very spare way. He does not tell of the Sanhedrin meeting, though it is implied in the sentence, "Annas then sent him bound to Caiaphas the high priest" (v. 24). The other writers have already narrated this hasty trial (Luke 22:66-71). Recent studies have shown that in Jerusalem the end of the third watch (3 A.M.) was signaled by the blowing of a trumpet and that this signal was popularly called the *cockcrow*. If Jesus was referring to this signal in his statement to Peter, then we may place Peter's denial at the close of the nighttime questioning of Jesus at the palace of the high priest's home, at about 3 A.M. (Some scholars feel that Annas and Caiaphas occupied different wings of the same palace, perhaps the Hasmonean Palace on the west hill of the city of Jerusalem. See Brown, *Gospel According to John*, p. 823).

We conclude from all the accounts that from about 3 A.M. to 6 A.M. the Sanhedrin met at Caiaphas's house, and then at about 6 A.M. —as John says, at "the early hour," daybreak—"they led Jesus . . . to the praetorium."

The term *praetorium* is used in the first century to describe the residence of the chief representative of Rome in Roman territory. The permanent residence of the Roman Governor was not at Jerusalem but at Caesarea (see Acts 33:33). During the Jewish holidays, for obvious administrative reasons, the governor would visit at Jerusalem. The question is—where does Pilate stay during his visits to Jerusalem. Two sites have been suggested: either the great Herodian Palace on the West Hill, built by Herod the Great in 23 B.C. ; or the Hasmonean Castle, called the Antonia Fortress, which Herod the Great had used as his palace from 35 to 23 B.C. At the site of the Antonia Fortress archeologists in 1870 discovered a pavement floor with massive stone slabs, each of which is more than one foot thick. The area measures some 2,300 square yards. Some of the stones have scratched into them games played by Roman soldiers. Most archeologists feel they were in place at the time of the first century. Therefore the Antonia Fortress is the most obvious site.

The accusers from the Sanhedrin do not enter the house of the Roman governor, in order not to suffer defilement on the eve of the holy Feast of Passover. We are not told by John what is the possible nature of the defilement. It may be the strict requirement that in the time of this feast of unleavened bread, Jews were not to have contact with leaven (Deut. 16:4). Therefore they would not enter a Gentile house during these days because of the presence of leaven.

"So Pilate came out to them" (v. 29). The fact that John does not identify Pilate to his readers as the procurator gives us another clue to John's awareness that his readers have available to them the other Gospel records. Matthew had identified Pilate more fully —"Jesus stood before the governor" (Matt. 27:11). Pilate is a well-attested historical figure, whose term as governor lasted from A.D. 26 to 36. Josephus, Philo and Tacitus each make extensive comments about him.

Pilate's position as procurator of Judea is not comfortable, and most of his reign is stormy. The special relationship between the house of Herod and Caesar has been well established. That friendship is a problem for Pilate and contributed to the reversal by Rome of several of his decisions and acts. There is also the considerable wealth and power of the house of Annas. "The family of Annas is mentioned several times in later Jewish writings; it was noted for its greed, as well as for its wealth and power" (R. E. Brown, p. 82). There is also the politically hazardous fact that the Jewish people are highly organized and have councils (i.e., the Sanhedrin) which have effectively organized the people. Another problem is the presence of extremist groups such as the Essenes, of whom we know a great deal now in light of the discoveries at Qumram. The Zealot party also pose a real and ever-present danger of uprising and disorder.

Add to this the feasts of the people which each year celebrate the liberation of Israel from the bondage of Egypt (Passover), the giving of God's Law which sets the people free from false law (Feast of Pentecost), the preservation of the people in their flight from Egypt to the promised land (Feast of Tabernacles), and the cleansing of the temple of the foreign oppressors and their false gods (Feast of Dedication). It is clear that these yearly feasts are a grave potential danger when thousands of the faithful gather in Jerusalem to celebrate their liberation from oppression. We can appreciate the high volatility of the week before Passover and the sense of danger that Pilate must feel, even though he will try to keep up the face of indifference and unruffled authority.

Pilate's role in the drama of Holy Week and his part in the trial and condemnation of Jesus seals the universal nature of the death of Jesus Christ. It is not just a Sanhedrin affair, not simply one more instance of capricious Roman oppression, not even a sudden emotional lynching of an angry mob.

Pilate at first seeks to return Jesus to the jurisdiction of the council. However, they refuse, since their request is the death sentence. John gives us the information that capital punishment is beyond the authority of the Sanhedrin. He alone of the Gospel writers gives us this important explanation: "It is not lawful for us to put any man to death." The most recent research into Roman policies indicates that John has given us an accurate account of the situation as of A.D. 30. One ancient Jewish document tells of the fact that "jurisdiction over life was taken from Israel forty years before the temple was destroyed" (C. K. Barrett, p. 445; R. E. Brown, p. 850). This would mean that at about A.D. 30, Rome limited such power and held the right of capital punishment to itself. John then makes the observation that because of this restraint, Jesus was not stoned, as Jewish law provided, but crucified, as was the practice of the Romans. In this terrible punishment the prophecy of Jesus was fulfilled: "And I, when I am lifted up from the earth, will draw all men to myself " (John 12:32).

Pilate then returns to the Praetorium, taking Jesus into the building with him, and leaving the accusers outside. Only John gives us this evidence of the private encounters between Pilate and Jesus, away from the others. In this brief dialogue, Jesus tells Pilate that his kingship is not of this world. Jesus accepts Pilate's statement: "So you are a king?" But the answer of Jesus is not an easy one for Pilate to understand: "for this I have come into the world, to bear witness to the truth." Pilate cuts off the conversation with his comment, "What is truth?" This is not so much a question by Pilate but a put down! He is not interested in ideology at a time like this. It is the furthest thing from his present interest.

Pilate then goes out to the accusers and seeks to release Jesus. He refers to a tradition in which a prisoner is released at Passover. The Gospels are our principal source of information concerning this tradition, though we have evidence that Roman governors did practice amnesty on occasions. Pilate asks them, "Will you have me release for you the King of the Jews?" We cannot be sure if Pilate's title is an example of his own cynical humor or his simple comment of who Jesus has been said to be.

The people shout out, "Not this man, but Barabbas." This other man, John tells us, was a highwayman, a bandit.

In Pilate's mind he does not see any connection between "the truth" and the dangerous historical situation with which he is uniquely faced and about which he alone must make a decision. For him truth is a philosophical luxury, and when Jesus brings it into focus, Pilate abruptly changes the subject. From that moment forward it is clear that Pilate is only able to decide on the basis of expediency and power, on the basis of where the power is and not upon the question of what is just or true. When the moment of decision confronts him, it is obvious that the way of justice requires time, time for Pilate as a judge to weigh and to think, but that to take that time requires tremendous inner strength and courage in the face of a potential riot. Pilate does not have that courage, and therefore, at the greatest crossroad moment of his life, he makes an awesome decision based upon the show of immediate power and the preservation of self-interest.

The dialogue between Jesus and this Roman official has placed squarely onto the stage of human history the great tension present at the moment of all important moral decisions. It is the tension between truth and power. Of the two, power has all of the immediate advantages. It is the power of the crowd that takes away from Pilate the necessary time to think. It is the power of Pilate that makes him think he is able to set aside the question of truth. The decisive moment only takes a few seconds' time, but the consequences will last throughout all time.

William Shirer tells in *The Rise and Fall of the Third Reich* of a meeting called by Herman Goering on the day following the country-wide mob violence against Jewish merchants. At that time he was economic czar in Germany. Insurance executives were told by Goering at that meeting that they would not be required to pay casuality losses to Jewish shopkeepers who had had their buildings attacked by young Nazi zealots the night before. Those executives faced the very crisis that Pilate faced—between, on the one side, justice that is apparently so weak and vulnerable and therefore so costly to embrace and, on the other side, power which is swift and immediately profitable to those who are in its favor.

Pilate must choose.

*The tragedy of Pontius Pilate is
that he must defend himself instead
of justice.*

37. Ecce Homo
John 19:1–16

John is careful to preserve for us the complex nature of the man
Pilate and the evolution of his decision. Pilate finds no crime in
Jesus worthy of death. He allows his soldiers to scourge Jesus and
mock him, perhaps in the hope that such severe punishment would
satisfy those who are against Jesus. Of the three forms of Roman
beatings, the scourge is usually a part of capital punishment.
There is ancient evidence that gives examples of mockery of condemned prisoners as also a part of punishment.

Luke tells us that at this point in the trial, Jesus is sent by Pilate
to Herod, who then sends him back, still leaving the matter for Pilate to decide. Once again in the private chamber, Pilate seeks to
find some solution. He says to Jesus, "Do you not know that I have
power to release you?" Jesus says to Pilate that those who have
brought him to Pilate have the greater sin.

Earlier in this Gospel Jesus had implied degrees of sin and guilt
in direct proportion to the light that a person had or claimed to
have. Jesus makes this teaching clear in his dialogue with some of
the Pharisees, following the healing of the man born blind. "Some
of the Pharisees ... said ... 'Are we also blind?' Jesus said to
them, 'If you were blind, you would have no guilt; but now that you
say 'We see,' your guilt remains' " (John 9:40–41).

John again tells the readers that Pilate wanted to release Jesus,
but the charge against Jesus now shifts to become a charge against
Pilate. The leaders from the house of Annas know the Roman
governor very well, and this new accusation is the most persuasive:
"If you release this man, you are not Caesar's friend; everyone who
makes himself a king sets himself against Caesar" (v. 12). Research
into the first-century period has shown that the term "friend of
Caesar" was in fact a technical title of honor of which only a handful of Roman leaders could boast. These accusers have found the

157

mark. No longer do they accuse Jesus; they now accuse Pilate, and of the worst of all failures—of not being true as a friend of Caesar. This charge is especially effective with a person who is basically unsure of himself and of his relationship to the highest source of authority he knows.

It is for this crime that Jesus will be crucified: he threatened the power of Caesar and the already shaky position of a Roman governor in Judea.

Since the time of Pilate, many men and women have discovered that to defend an unpopular person from injustice almost always results in the hatred of the crowd and inevitably results in the shift of attack from the accused to the person who dares to defend him. At that moment, only the person who has a source of justice and meaning beyond the immediate rewards and relationships of present power is able to withstand the charge: You are not "Caesar's friend."

Jean Paul Sartre, the atheist and Marxist, has written a strange sentence in his book *Words:* "I only trust in those who only trust in God." Pilate is no match for his accusers, because they have found his small god by which he pragmatically solves every question, every equation.

John tells that at about the sixth hour Pilate won a meager victory for Rome from a preoccupied crowd, when they said, "We have no king but Caesar." Then Pilate handed Jesus over to be crucified. Mark's record is as follows: "And it was the third hour, when they crucified him" (Mark 15:25). John gives a different time in his narrative: "It was about the sixth hour." Some interpreters have tried to harmonize this difference in time notation by the suggestion that John has made use of a different starting point in his hour computation. I feel that the best approach is to resist artificial harmonizations but rather to allow the texts to stand as they are written. It is impressive to note that the early church was unwilling to force the two texts into harmony. It may seem ironic to some, but this very difference in narrative detail actually further endorses the integrity of the documents and their transmission to us.

There was a brief and terrifying moment for Pilate when the people thought he was a friend of Jesus. They quickly convinced him that such a friendship with Jesus posed a danger to that other friendship that meant so much to Pilate. The chances are that Caesar hardly knew his representative in Judea.

38. The Humiliation of Jesus
John 19:17–30

John's narrative of the death of Jesus is brief, yet thoughtful and sensitive. There is an understatement about these sentences that is deeply moving and made the more so by their reserve and simplicity. Once again, as throughout the Gospel, there is an attention to detail and to the names of people. John chooses not to repeat some of the incidents and words from the cross that the other Gospel writers have already narrated.

John tells us that Jesus carried his own cross. Luke tells of the man Simon who was forced to help Jesus. The destination was a hill called, "Place of a skull." John first gives his Greek readers the name in Greek, and then adds the name it was known by to the people of Jerusalem. *Golgotha* means skull in Hebrew. In Latin, skull is *calvaria*, hence the name we use in English—Mt. Calvary. Where is this place today? Most archeologists favor the site at or near where the present Church of the Holy Sepulchre stands.

John then writes, "There they crucified him and with him two others." He gives none of the brutal details of this most horrible punishment by which a human being was not only executed but was deprived of all human dignity. Crucifixion was slow death of dehydration and fatigue. It was emotional as well as physical execution. Josephus calls crucifixion, "the most wretched of deaths," and Cicero, "most cruel and terrible punishment." Each Gospel tells of the other prisoners and Luke tells of the word of Jesus to the one who asked for help. Each writer tells of the inscription placed on the cross. Matthew tells us it was placed over the head of Jesus. Only John tells us that the inscription was at the express instruction of Pilate, and that it was written in Greek, Latin and Hebrew. We have evidence that it was a practice in Roman crucifixion to publish the charge against a condemned prisoner. The wording of the inscription is reported in slightly different form by

159

each Gospel writer. John alone reports that the town of Jesus is included: "Jesus of Nazareth, the King of the Jews." John gives us another detail—the attempt of representatives of the high priests to have the inscription changed. Finally Pilate stands firm: "What I have written I have written."

John then tells of the soldiers gambling for the seamless tunic of Jesus. It was a Roman custom that the soldiers were entitled to the clothing of condemned prisoners, since in Roman crucifixion the condemned person was stripped of his clothing. John does not write bitterly of this cynical act; instead he remembers and quotes from Psalm 22—the very psalm from which Jesus cried out in the language of his youth, "Eloi, Eloi, lama sabach-thani?" "My God, my God, why hast thou forsaken me?" (Matt. 27:46; Mark 15:34).

Then John records a word from the cross which he alone has preserved for us. Jesus speaks first to Mary his mother and then to the beloved disciple who we believe is John. He commits them to each other. There is a simplicity and tenderness about these words that gives to us one more vital insight into Jesus.

Four women are present at the cross according to John: Mary the mother of Jesus, his mother's sister, Mary wife of Clopas, and Mary Magdalene. The final few sentences relate words of Jesus "I thirst"—"I am thirsty." Once again, note John's interpretation of his Lord's inner feelings and convictions: "After this, aware that all was now finished, in order to bring the scripture to its complete fulfillment Jesus said . . ." (v. 28, literal).

John records an act of kindness by the soldiers who offer some common wine on a sponge to Jesus. The RSV translates the word *oxos* as "vinegar," but this may be misleading to most English speaking readers. The word refers to a wine that was commonly drunk by soldiers. Mark and Matthew tell of a mixture of wine and gall/myrrh which was supposed to have a narcotic effect, but this first drink, according to Mark and Matthew, Jesus refused to drink. When Jesus took the wine, "he said, 'It is finished'; and he bowed his head and gave up his spirit."

Now we must ask the question; What is the meaning of the death of Jesus Christ? The principal interpretive sentence is verse 28: "After this, aware that all was now finished, in order to bring the scripture to its complete fulfillment . . ." In order to understand its meaning, we must seek to trace Jesus' explicit statements recorded throughout this Gospel, as well as John's comments, and even the testimony about Jesus sometimes from unlikely and strange sources (i.e., Caiaphas in the council: "one must die for the nation").

We find at least three major themes converging to help us understand what has happened at Mt. Calvary.

(1) First, Jesus Christ fulfills the Old Testament expectation for a Savior who would take the people's place. Sacrificial animals symbolically represented this expectation in the feast of Passover and on Yom Kippur. Caiaphas had said that one person must die for the people (John 11:50). Though these words were meant to solidify a conspiracy against Jesus, yet they are a true witness to who Jesus is. He is the one who dies on behalf of the people.

Jesus has said this of himself: "I am the good shepherd. The good shepherd lays down his life for the sheep" (John 10:11). Jesus has made a total identification with the people as the suffering servant portrayed in Isaiah 53. That Isaiah text had promised that "with his stripes we are healed." This theme is also taught by Jesus when he illustrates his mission to Nicodemus from the incident of the children of Israel in the wilderness: "as Moses lifted up the serpent in the wilderness, so must the Son of man be lifted up, that whoever believes in him may have eternal life" (John 3:14, 15).

The basic point is that we do not have within ourselves the resources to resolve this deepest of all human crises—our sinfulness which leads to our death. Dietrich Bonhoeffer has put it in the terms of our own intensely personal crisis—"We cannot confer forgiveness upon ourselves" (*Cost of Discipleship*, p. 36). In recognition of this profound fact, the dramas of sacrifice become a vital part each year in the life of Israel. Each feast in the year recognized the need of Israel for God as the only Redeemer. Now John tells us that the yearnings present in these dramas have all come to their completion, not symbolically, but actually, just outside the city of Jerusalem.

(2) "Greater love hath no man than this, that a man lay down his life for his friends" (John 15:13). These words by Jesus tell us that the reason for the death of Jesus in behalf of the world is his love for us. Jesus is the shepherd who cares for the sheep and knows them by name (John 10). "For God so loved the world that he gave his only son," Jesus told Nicodemus. The love that we have observed throughout John's portrayal of the life of Jesus Christ: the love that finds the broken people like the Samaritan woman, the man at the Bethesda pool, the man born blind; the love that was moved to tears at the grief of Martha and Mary; the love that cared so deeply about the disciples and their feelings that he walked across the lake in a storm to come to them, that he washed their dirty feet—this love of Jesus Christ is the reason for

the event at Calvary. This love preserved the freedom of the disciples and allowed them to fail. At the death of Jesus this love is revealed in its richest colors; at his resurrection it will shine in its brightest colors. It is love as event ultimate and concretely real.

(3) But there is one more profoundly important thing that happens on Good Friday. Jesus is disarming the power of sin, death and the devil by taking into his own hand the cup of death: "Shall I not drink the cup . . . .?" (18:11). There is a battle being waged at Mt. Calvary that is of far graver significance than we men and women of history can fathom. I believe this is why John shifts the attention in his narrative of the final hours of Jesus' life away from the people and the accusers. John gives us no accounting of those who come to the cross to taunt and mock Jesus, as if the battle were really at last between people and Jesus. Certainly those things happened; our own experiences in this century have shown us that crowds of people are eager to watch a public execution. But Jesus Christ is battling evil itself. "Now is the judgment of this world, now shall the ruler of this world be cast out; and I, when I am lifted up from the earth, will draw all men to myself" (John 12:31–32). Later in the last discourse he said, "The ruler of this world is coming. He has no power over me" (John 14:30). The fury of evil must be met and taken in order to disarm it. It must be *judged;* that is, it must be revealed and exposed. Only as we see the greater power of God's love alongside the deadly power of evil are we set free from our fear of evil.

This is the subjective truth in Christ's victory at Mt. Calvary. "In the world you have tribulation; but be of good cheer, I have overcome the world" (John 16:33). But the Gospel intends an objective victory as well. Jesus wins the actual victory. It is concrete and real. Therefore, when John heard our Lord's great shout, "Finished," he realized the deepest truth in that shout. Evil has spent its best weapons—all the same ones we experience, though in lesser force—but Jesus has taken them all upon himself. The full weight of evil is very heavy on Friday, because Jesus is dead.

39. Jesus Is Dead
John 19:31–42

John presents now to his readers more information not found in the other Gospels. He tells us that Jewish leaders went to Pilate to request that the condemned and dying men be killed before sunset. The Jews are a humane people with a humane legal tradition. In that tradition they could not allow a condemned person to be left hanging overnight (Deut. 21:22–23). Research into Roman practices shows that usually a corpse was left hanging upon a cross for several days, probably to stand as a warning to criminals. However, Josephus tells that the Romans made an exception in this policy in the case of the Jews. This is the meaning of the request that the legs of those who were crucified that day be broken in order to hasten death.

John reports this grim, though necessary, part of his account in a way that shifts our attention from the soldiers carrying out their brutal work to its meaning. He puts the event into the context of two Old Testament texts which had told that his bones would not be broken but that his side would be pierced (Exod. 12:46; Zech. 12:10). John bears his own personal witness that Jesus' side was pierced, "and at once there came out blood and water" (John 19:34).

It is important to John that his readers know of the actual fact of death. Jesus did not simply appear to die. The death of Jesus is as real as his life. Jesus is not a phantom who evaded the humiliation of that dark Friday.

The final paragraph tells the details of the burial of Jesus. The secret disciple, Joseph of Arimathea—a man from a small town in Judea—and Nicodemus the Pharisee together arrange for as decent burial as is possible on the eve of Passover.

We naturally are led to ask of this part of John's account why he is so insistent upon the fact of the death of Jesus. "He who saw it has borne witness—his testimony is true, and he knows that he tells the truth" (v. 35).

It is my understanding of the text that John is not insisting upon the truthfulness of what he saw, as if *water and blood* were a miracle he had witnessed. This has been a view expressed by some commentators. Rather John is insisting upon the real death of Jesus Christ which the spear wound and the body fluids and blood proved.

All New Testament writers insist that Jesus really died—that his humiliation was complete. It is part of their affirmation over against the protognostic spiritualization of Jesus into a holy representative who is not fully human and therefore does not really die but only appears to die. It may be possible that at the time of John's writing of the Gospel he is aware of these protognostic teachings, and therefore we have this eye-witness verification of the humanity of Jesus. It is as important to John that Jesus is flesh as it is to him that Jesus is ultimate Word.

This narrative has now posed a great crisis for all who have followed seriously these records of the words and works of Jesus Christ.

Jesus Christ made such great promises: "If anyone thirst let him come unto me . . . I am the bread of life . . . Neither do I condemn you . . . Peace I leave with you, my peace I give unto you . . ." What are we to do with these promises? Do we dare build our lives upon them? How can we count upon the promises of Jesus, now that we know of his crushing defeat at Mt. Calvary?

Everything is now at the crossroads. The people of Jesus face only a few major options. There is the way of nihilistic despair. This is Judas's choice when the full reality of his betrayal comes in upon him. He destroys his life. There is also the way of panic, regret and confusion. This is the way of the eleven disciples.

There is another way too—the way of respectful honor shown to a heroic but fallen friend. This is the way of the women, of Joseph of Arimathea and of Nicodemus. They bury Jesus with dignity, and after the Holy Day is over, the women plan to properly prepare his body for burial.

As things stand at the close of chapter 19 in John's Gospel, there are really no other options. Certainly the words of Jesus are memorable and haunting, but they are words to be honored, not proclaimed.

Johann Sebastian Bach has caught the mood of that Friday evening in a great chorus of the *Passion according to St. Matthew:*

Ah! Golgotha? unhappy Golgotha!
The Lord of Glory here beneath a curse is lying;
He hangs upon the accursed tree,
Who shall the world's Redeemer be;
The Lord Who heaven and earth created
By earth is now reviled and hated;
The sinless, lo, for sin is dying;
With stricken soul the sight I see.

40. On the First Day

John 20:1-23

We know from many first-century evidences that the message about the resurrection of Jesus Christ from the dead was a fundamental part of the gospel of the primitive church. That word spread throughout the Mediterranean world wherever the Christians were to go. These people believed that the victory had been won by Jesus over death itself, and this conviction was the central part of their preaching. (Wolfhart Pannenberg's *Jesus, God and Man* is a recent study of these early evidences.)

Each Gospel writer and the writers of the New Testament letters affirm that victory, and they celebrate its implications. Because of that event, Christians soon were worshiping together on the first day of the week as well as on the Sabbath.

Now let us observe John's record of the event that sustained the church's faith.

John's account begins with the early morning visit to the grave by Mary Magdalene. Each Gospel tells of the women at the tomb early on the first day, but each has a different list of names. What is certain, thought is that women are the first to discover the victory of Jesus Christ over death, and they are the first to preach the gospel to the world.

As I have observed earlier, the differences in names and small details of sequences do not damage for us, some two thousand years later, the historical trustworthiness of the Gospel writers. In fact, our historical suspicions would be more aroused if a swift-moving incident such as this one had been reported by each writer with identical detail. Here, therefore, is another gain for us as historians when we see these differences of account in our basic documents. It shows to us, on the one hand, that the early handlers and copiers of these Gospel records did not alter the records to harmonize the narratives. It is remarkable how relatively few additions to the original documents have been made in manuscripts by the early preservers and copiers. It also shows us that each Gospel writer makes his own witness. The public information section of the church does not then later harmonize the records so that there can be no possible misinterpretation. We would expect this of propaganda and public relations releases. The Gospels, however, are witness documents, written to express truthfully what the writers themselves saw or heard from other witnesses to be the event as it really happened.

According to John, Mary Magdalene discovers that the stone has been rolled back. Mark (15:46) and Matthew (28:60) also tell of this stone against the opening. Mary suspects that someone has stolen the body, and she runs to Simon Peter—and we presume John (in this passage the two autographs are used together—"the other disciple, the one whom Jesus loved"). These two disciples and Mary Magdalene run back to the tomb. John, the younger man, arrives first but stays outside the tomb. Peter then leads John into the tomb, and the two are convinced that the body is not there. They suspect, as does Mary, the theft of the body. While Peter and John go back to the city, Mary stays by the deserted grave site weeping. She sees two messengers in white who ask her why she is crying. "Because they have taken away my Lord, and I do not know where they have laid him."

Mary then sees Jesus, but John tells us that she did not know it was he and supposes that he is a gardener. He also asks her why she is crying and whom she is looking for. She asks for help in finding Jesus' body: "Sir, if you have carried him away, tell me where you have laid him, and I will take him away." Jesus speaks to her one word and that word breaks through the wall of her grief and despair. It is her own name. He will later assure her of *his* name and of his kingly reign, but the first confirmation of Jesus Christ's triumph by Jesus himself begins with this simple dialogue.

It seems odd at first glance that Mary should have been confirmed in the living reality of Jesus because her name was spoken, not his. In fact, this is how most confirmations of the living Christ take place. There is no one who knows us as well and as deeply as the one who made us and redeems us. It should not then be strange that he most deeply proves himself to us by showing us to ourselves.

Mary returns to proclaim this event to the disciples: "I have seen the Lord." The disciples evidently do not believe her. Luke gives us this report of the reaction of the disciples to the affirmation of the women: "But these words seemed to them idle talk and they did not believe them" (Luke 24:11).

On this Sunday after Passover, the disciples, except for Thomas, have gathered together in a locked room. Suddenly, "Jesus came and stood among them and said to them, 'Peace be with you.' " Jesus had spoken the word *peace* at the close of his Thursday night discourse: "I have said this to you, that in me you may have peace . . . " (John 16:33). Now it is the word he speaks when he meets his disciples after his death. *Shalom* is the rich Hebrew word that Jesus may have spoken. It is a common greeting among Jews, whereas among Greeks the common greeting would be *chara* —joy. *Shalom* means more than the absence of conflict: it means health, wholeness, salvation.

Jesus shows to his disciples the marks of his death. "Then the disciples were glad when they saw the Lord." They have been set free to celebrate, and this joyous note is to be a mark of the Christians. Because Christ has really won the victory there is cause for genuine rejoicing. But this does not mean that Christians become escapists. This very Gospel gives us evidence that Jesus Christ has serious plans for his followers. Let us seek to trace them in the experiences of Easter.

The result of the victory of Jesus Christ is the joyous assurance given by Christ to the disciples personally: "Mary," "Peace." First, Jesus finds his disciples. Second, he assures them of the reality of his victory: "he showed them his hands." Third, he gives them the great commission. This commission sends them into the real world as his representatives. "As the father has sent me, even so I send you" (20:21). John tells us that having said this, and before completing the instructions of his commission, Jesus "breathed on them, and said to them, 'Receive the Holy Spirit' . . ."

The ministry of the Holy Spirit is twofold: first to convict me of my need of Christ (John 16), and then to assure my heart and mind of the reality of Jesus Christ as Lord. In this assurance the Holy Spirit companions and equips me by continuing ministry in my life and in the lives of my brothers and sisters in Christ. When I am able to say that Jesus Christ is my Lord and to feel assured of that relationship, it is because the Holy Spirit has convinced my mind and heart. Therefore it is relationship language that describes the biblical portrait of the ministry of the Holy Spirit.

Jesus also promises authority to his disciples. Power for the Christian is our confidence that Jesus Christ is Lord and that he reigns and has the power. The ministry of the Holy Spirit is portrayed in John's Gospel in very personal language and the result of the Holy Spirit's ministry is the creation of a missionary body, the church. "He breathed on them."

This moment in the life of the disciples and the event at Pentecost are experiences of assurance for them that Jesus Christ is Lord indeed, and that he has won the victory over death. Therefore, his promises made during his ministry in Galilee and Judea are sealed. They are authoritative. We who live many years later may build upon them, and we may proclaim them to the world.

At the very heart of Jesus' great commission to his disciples stand this act and the brief sentence which shifts our attention away from the disciples and their task to the great reality which is prior to them and their task. Now we know that the disciples are not the gospel. We do not have one gospel in the first nineteen chapters of John which tells of Jesus and what he did, followed by a second gospel which is about the disciples and their important commission in the world.

In my view, Rudolf Bultmann has erred both historically and theologically at this point. In effect, the valiant faith of the primitive church becomes for him the real gospel to which we in our century look. But such a shift in focus means that we have become our own good news. The danger in such a shift is that the gospel becomes subjectively variable; we are continuously tempted to idealize any current cause or prophetic concern as if it were the gospel. The revolution for social justice may then become the gospel; or perhaps the special experiences of Christians in their pilgrimage of faith may become the gospel; or our gospel may turn out to be the safe status quo preservation of a certain favorite theme or establishment. But, in fact, this is a misunderstanding of the New Testament. When Jesus breathed upon the disciples, he bound them to himself and his reign. Their authority flows out of and depends upon the gospel. His gospel will be the check and balance upon the ministry of the disciples for all time. The Holy Spirit will not lead the disciples toward new doctrines about new gospels but rather will "bring to your remembrance all that I have said to you" (John 14:25).

Jesus gives to his followers serious responsibility in the world: "if you forgive the sins of any ... if you retain the sins ..." This sentence about the mission of the disciples is not an easy one to interpret. Both sides of the parallel sentence pose interpretative problems, especially if the sentence is not seen within its larger context. What is clear is that the disciples are invited by Jesus Christ to share the good news of forgiveness in the world; the text tells us that "any one" may receive this forgiveness of sin. Jesus brushes aside any concern that there might be sinners too far gone so that for them there could be no hope. The disciples are instructed to extend the forgiveness *in behalf of Christ*—"I send you." Therefore we conclude that in no way does this commission to the disciples give to them original authority or privilege. The role of the disciples is serious but not ultimate; it is Jesus Christ who forgives. Therefore the disciples, since they have received the Holy Spirit who binds them to Christ, do not become in themselves the Savior. Their authority is derived from Jesus Christ who commissions them and who breathes on them.

The theological problem in this sentence is that a certain reading of the sentence without any contextual restraint may lead a reader to find such a degree of authority granted to the disciples that we are embarrassed by its scope and apparent unchallenged completeness. The second part of the sentence's parallelism is also problematic: "If you hold the sins they are held." The question is this: Just how much authority has Jesus here given to his followers? Matthew helps us with this question in his record of the great commission. In his narrative, it is clear that Jesus in no way compromises his own authority as he grants authority to his followers: "All authority in heaven and on earth has been given to me. Go therefore and make disciples . . . , and lo, I am with you always to the close of the age" (Matt 28:18–20).

My own conclusion is to allow this sentence to stand as it is—a commission to the disciples to face seriously their task in the world, which is to live out and share the reality of forgiveness. There is a mysterious sense in which the disciples of Jesus Christ participate in the world's chance to know of the gospel. The disciples have real responsibility but not the ultimate responsibility, because it stands in a lower position to the authority of Christ.

*Thomas's doubts about the resurrec-
tion are not discounted but are resolved when he recognizes the
Risen Christ as the Jesus he has
known.*

41. Thomas the Twin

John 20:24–29

Thomas was not with the disciples on that first Sunday when
Jesus appeared. But when they tell him of their experience—"We
have seen the Lord"—Thomas is not able to believe their witness
to him. Only John's Gospel records this incident. Thomas does not
doubt the person, Jesus; he doubts the witness to the victory of
Jesus. Jesus he loves, and Jesus he is willing to follow, but all that
he has to build on at this point in his journey of faith is the witness
of his friends that they have seen the Lord. Thomas is still uncertain, and therefore he stipulates to these friends important
conditions that for him must be satisfied. "Unless I see in his
hands . . . "

I believe that what Thomas is saying is this: "I have followed
Jesus for three years. I have heard his words and seen his acts. I
know that this man Jesus was slain on Golgotha and that death is
the most real fact of all for me. I will believe in *that* man if he is
alive!" That is the significance as I see it of Thomas's criteria. He
will not settle for faith that is founded upon any other foundation:
not the hopes of the disciples, now possibly fantasized into a phantom dream, not even angelic or spiritual proof. Thomas will only
believe in Jesus of Nazareth if he is alive. The matter is crucial to
him, and therefore he sets out conditions to that end. In theological terms, Thomas is insisting that the *Jesus of history* and the
Christ of faith must be one and the same. He will not believe in
the Christ of faith who is not also the actual Jesus whom he had
known and trusted.

"Eight days later, his disciples were again in the house and
Thomas was with them." Though Thomas is basically unresolved
and unsure about the affirmation of the other disciples, nevertheless they resist the temptation to purge this doubter from their fellowship. This willingness to wait it out with Thomas reveals their

171

confidence in Christ and his actual victory. At the same time, Thomas's willingness to stay with the disciples honestly and without any false statements—he does not seek to please them with hypocrisy—is a tribute to the integrity both of Thomas and of the other disciples.

On this occasion Jesus greets Thomas as he had greeted the others: "Peace be with you," and he offers the sign that Thomas had requested. However, John does not record that Thomas actually placed his hands upon the hand of Jesus. Instead, Thomas speaks the greatest affirmation in this gospel: "My Lord and my God!" Thomas does not need as many signs as he thought at first he did. Jesus Christ has found him where he is and now he is assured of the victory of the Jesus of history.

This incident closes with the words of Jesus: "Have you believed because you have seen me? Blessed are those who have not seen and yet believe." These words have been interpreted as a rebuke of Thomas's hesitancy to believe. I choose, however, to interpret the sentence as a simple declarative statement of fact. Thomas believes, and many disciples who will not have the visual sign that Thomas has experienced will also believe. In other words, the doubt of Thomas as it is resolved becomes a gain for countless men and women through the centuries since Thomas.

Because of Thomas, we know that at least one person among the founders of the primitive church had insisted that the Jesus of history and the Christ of faith be the same person. Thomas would only worship the Jesus who really died, and therefore his difficult journey to faith becomes for us a very vital theological ingredient in the formation of our understanding of the gospel. We now know that the historical question was indeed asked by the early Christians, just as we ask it in our generation. Christian faith does not worship a phantom Jesus, a fantasy Jesus; nor is it the brave faith of men and women about a memory about Jesus. We go the whole way—our faith is in the Jesus who lives.

Without the real victory of Jesus of Nazareth, there is no adequate reason for celebration, because Jesus promised too much. This is the critical weakness in every story about Jesus that refuses this radical center—the actual victory over death. Stephen Schwartz has written a joyous musical discovery of Jesus in the Broadway musical *Godspell*. But he evades the resurrection of Jesus. Because he is fearful of this most radical center, he must evade the really decisive teaching of Jesus. The joy that is in the musical is turned into play. The element of the genuine tragedy of the cross has also been lost. We don't understand the depths of

Jesus' love, though we do catch a glimpse, because it is impossible to miss the greatness of Jesus even when the study of his life is itself superficial.

This Gospel is an earnest narrative of events. John honestly tells his readers that his purpose in writing is to encourage those who read to believe that "Jesus is the Christ."

John is not a storyteller who has started with a dogma and then has worked backward to create the marvelous stories about Jesus that we have read. The documents just don't read that way. The critics who too quickly endorsed that approach to the interpretation of John have missed the opportunity to grapple with the words and events in this Gospel simply on their own merits. It has been their loss.

The most famous pupil of Rudolf Bultmann has been forced recently to reevaluate that methodology: "I now return to our starting point. Even if Bultmann's hypothesis is the right one, there would still be no sufficient motivation for the writing of the Gospels. . . . For Bultmann . . . the writing of the Gospels remains in the last resort an incomprehensible and superfluous sport in the natural history of the Kerygma" (Ernst Käsemann, *New Testament Questions of Today*, p. 57).

But for those who have allowed the Gospel to be the document that it claims to be—a serious narrative of the event, Jesus Christ—they have discovered that the Gospel of John has drawn them into the history of Jesus and to the crossroads where we must choose.

42. The Intimate Gospel
John 21:1–25

The Gospel seems to close with the verses of 20:30–31, but now we encounter another chapter. Manuscript evidence fully supports the inclusion of this chapter. The literary analysis of its form supports its authorship by the same author as chapters 1–20. Nevertheless, the chapter has been questioned by many New Testament scholars. Some have wanted to change its sequential position; others have credited a redactor adding this postscript later; others conclude that the chapter was written by Luke to harmonize the Gospel of John with the Synoptic accounts. All of these hypotheses have difficulty, however, because there simply is no adequate evidence present in the material itself or in manuscript research to justify any of them.

The most logical literary conclusion is to accept the chapter as it stands in our text—as an epilogue to the book. John is not the only New Testament author who thought he had concluded a book and then finding another theme come to mind, like a great jet about to land suddenly aborts the proposed landing and again roars into the sky with just a few more things to say. The Apostle Paul is about to draw his Philippian letter to a simple close in chapter 3:1, "Finally, my brethren . . . " Suddenly he thinks of evil workers at large in Macedonia and, changing his plan, writes two more chapters. Romans 15:33 closes that great letter: "The God of peace be with you all. Amen." Yet the apostle then proceeds to devote twenty-seven more sentences to the people he knows in Rome, including his quotation of perhaps an early church creed (16:25–26; see E. F. Palmer, *Salvation by Surprise*, pp. 175 ff.) There is precedent, therefore, for a New Testament writer to apparently conclude, only to continue with one more instruction, one more event, or as in the case of John, with a postscript or epilogue.

It is very much like the John we know in this Gospel—the one who has noticed the small details—to be compelled in his mind to write just one more important scene. We observe in the final sentence of the chapter a note of humor precisely to this point: "But there are also many other things which Jesus did; were every one of them to be written, I suppose that the world itself could not contain the books that would be written." This interesting sentence is appropriate at the close of a postscript. John does not attempt another theological and devotional ending—he has already done that in chapter 20.

What then happens in this epilogue? John has only narrated Judean appearances of the risen Jesus, and now he recalls for his readers an incident in Galilee.

"Peter said to them 'I am going fishing.'" Some interpreters find it difficult to imagine that the disciples, after two memorable encounters with Jesus in Judea and having heard his command to go into the world, would then waste time fishing in Galilee. I am not so sure! It takes time for the pieces to fit together in a person's life, especially if the way of discipleship has freedom in it. Peter has experienced the victory of Christ and he is glad of that true event. But he had fallen hard in his denial of Jesus. It takes time for a person to resolve the feelings of depression that result from a moral defeat like denial. What can Peter do? In his own eyes, before himself, he is discredited, and though he may rejoice in the victory of Jesus, it takes more time for Christ's victory to become his victory.

It makes sense to me that Peter is doing what you and I would tend to do with feelings of loose ends. He returns to what he knows best and feels good about. He may not be a great man of faith, but a fisherman he is. It is my view that a depressed Peter decides to go fishing, and just as the disciples had stayed with Thomas through his battle for faith, so now they stay with a struggling Peter through his lonely battle.

"But that night they caught nothing." Usually the best fishing on the Lake of Galilee is at night. These fishermen, however, have gone through the night without a catch. In the early morning "Jesus stood on the beach . . . and said to them 'Children [lads], have you any fish?'" None of the disciples recognize him, but they answer no and then Jesus tells them, "Cast the net on the right side of the boat, and you will find some." They do so and enclose a large catch of fish.

It is John who recognizes who this person is and who tells Peter, "It is the Lord." Jesus has built a fire and has some fish already cooking and also bread. John even tells his readers the number of

fish in the catch—153. He is amazed that the net is not torn.
Through the centuries, interpreters of this event have endeavored
to find symbolism in the number 153. The result is a fanciful kind
of interpretation which in my view has the effect of trivializing the
narrative. These men are fishermen, and when the fish are big you
count them, especially if you are poor. The fact is that John likes
to note details which other narrators would ignore.

John tells us that the disciples are silent, so that it is Jesus who
speaks first. This silence of the disciples, along with their initial
nonrecognition of Jesus, is one of the marks of their total surprise
at the victory of their Lord. Details of this sort further encourage
our confidence in this trustworthiness of John's record. We would
expect a faith document to read differently, but John tells it like it
really was because his narrative is first of all a historical document
and only secondarily a dogmatic document.

Jesus asks Peter, "Simon, son of John, do you love me more than
these?" It is difficult to fix precisely what the pronoun "these" refers to. It is most likely, however, that the reference is to the fish
and fishing. Contextually, this is the most persuasive interpretation. Peter answers, "Yes, Lord, you know that I love you."

The oldest interpreters did not give special significance to the
changes in the word for love from Jesus' questions to Peter's answers. Later commentators have noted the significant change. Two
times Jesus asks Peter about his love, using the verb *agapas;* each
time Peter answers with the very personal friendship word *phileō.*
Finally, in the third question, Jesus asks the question with Peter's
word—*phileis.*

Has Jesus moved over to the vocabulary of Peter? If the dialogue between Peter and Jesus was in Aramaic, their native dialect, any distinction between the words they used would be unlikely. Though Jesus probably taught in Greek, especially while in
Judea, he probably used the common Galilean dialect when he and
the disciples were the only ones together. We cannot be certain in
this text.

The important thing to note is that three times Jesus confronts
Peter with a present-tense question and a present-tense commission. Jesus does not quiz his disciple about the failures of the past
but rather about Peter's decision in the present. Jesus Christ has
already resolved Peter's past, but Peter needs a threefold existential confrontation to make it clear to him. In this dialogue, Jesus
has therapeutically brought Peter firmly into the present. He then
places Peter once again into the key pastoral role among the disciples. He is to nurture the sheep that belong to Christ. Things are
right again.

Luke tells us that it was at a fishing incident where Jesus had first made sense to Peter. (Luke 5). (Luke's account is not a parallel account to this Johannine incident.) In that event, also at Galilee, Jesus had been teaching the people from the boat. "And when he had ceased speaking, he said to Simon, 'Put out into the deep and let down your nets for a catch.'" Peter argues with Jesus, protesting that they had fished all night and had caught nothing. But grudgingly Peter obeys what he considers the foolish suggestion of Jesus. "And when they had done this, they enclosed a great shoal of fish." Luke records for us Peter's reaction to the great catch. "But when Simon Peter saw it, he fell down at Jesus' knees, saying, "Depart from me, for I am a sinful man, O Lord."

Jesus had really won Peter to himself in that fishing incident. It was not so much through the words of his sermons, not even his signs—just a little earlier Jesus had healed Peter's mother-in-law—that reached Peter. Peter needed to meet Jesus in the *place* that he understood as well as to hear words that he understood. Two fishing incidents—one at the beginning and the other at the middle of Peter's Christian pilgrimage—are each important signposts in his life.

John has written this epilogue as a tribute to Peter, who would always be known in the history of the Christian church as *the Fisherman*—an honorable name for this great man. We owe a debt to John for having preserved for us two very personal and understandable portrayals: Thomas with his doubts that needed to be resolved and Peter with his lingering discouragement that also needed to be resolved. Jesus Christ is the Good Shepherd who *knows* his sheep and is able to find them where they really are and not where we wish they were. He now instructs Peter to be a shepherd too.

John then records a strange sentence by Jesus: "... when you were young, ... you walked where you would; but when you are old ... another will gird you and carry you where you do not wish to go." John follows this with his comment: "(This he said to show by what death he was to glorify God.)" Most interpreters agree that this sentence is the prophecy of Peter's death by crucifixion. A Christian epistle written from Christians at Rome to Christians at Corinth at the close of the first century or early in the second century tells of Peter's martyrdom (1 Clement 5:4), and there are references in the church fathers to the fact that Peter was crucified at Rome. But this hard prophecy is concluded with the words, "Follow me." The epilogue closes with one final scene.

Peter is now clearly the leader, and feeling a wave of authority coming over him, he notices for some reason the other disciple—John—and asks Jesus about him: "Lord, what about this man?" Jesus limits the authority of Peter and makes it very clear that Peter the shepherd is an undershepherd. "If it is my will that he remain until I come, what is that to you? Follow me!"

This scene provides one more window through which to see the true humanity of the disciples. They are just as human after the confirmation of the Holy Spirit as before. The heroes of the New Testament are not plastic personages created by mass media propagandists. They feel, worry, fear, love and believe as ordinary human beings.

Jesus is Lord, and he does not grant Peter an answer to this question. In the fifth book of C. S. Lewis's *Chronicles of Narnia, The Horse and His Boy*, the boy Shasta finally meets the great lion Aslan and learns from Aslan the amazing story of his own young life and Aslan's part in it. Aslan tells Shasta of the boy's beginnings, his journeys, and helps Shasta to understand what it all means. At that point Shasta asks Aslan to explain the meaning of some of the experiences of his traveling companion Aravis. Aslan answers: "I am telling you your story, not hers. I tell no-one any story but his own" (p. 159).

This final sentence of Jesus in the Gospel of John is a freedom sentence. It preserves his freedom as Lord and our freedom as disciples. John is free from the domination of Peter and Peter is free from the need to know everything about John. They belong to each other in Christ. Because of Christ we have mediated relationships with one another that preserve the dignity of each of us.

John then squashes a rumor that had evidently circulated among the churches that he, the beloved disciple, was not to die. John has no illusions of grandeur and he seeks no false honor. The book closes with his attestation. Perhaps, like Paul, he dictated the letter to a secretary and now takes the pen into his own hand to place a personal autograph at its close.

He has told us about Jesus Christ and the account is true. It is good news—as fresh and real today in our century as in the first century of our Lord.

Study Guide

Here are some study questions for individual and/or small group study of the Gospel of John, and a few suggestions regarding methods of study. First, read the text aloud, and then sentence by sentence begin your response to the book. I find it helpful to begin this response in the simplest way possible: How does the sentence strike me? Do words catch my attention? What do I feel at this stage of my enquiry is the main point being made? What are secondary points? After responding in this fashion, you are ready to expand your questioning to a consideration of what I would call the five principal questions that make up a commentary upon a biblical text. These questions, or doorways, into the content of the passage, are:

1) *The technical questions.* That is, what do the words mean? What is the best textual reading? What role does the grammatical structure play in the sentence, etc.?

2) *The historical questions.* These questions work at two levels primarily. First, historical curiosity that needs to be sharpened and aimed toward the setting and background of the textual material. If you meet a character such as John the Baptist, then the historical question is "Who is he?" If he is called "a baptizer," then the historical question is, "What does the term *baptism* mean in the context of the passage?"

There is also the second level at which the historical question is important, though more difficult to fasten down: What is the setting behind the text within the church at the time of the writing of the document? This historical question is very helpful in understanding *why* Paul may say what he says to the Galatians or the Philippians. In the Gospel of John this question enables us to wonder cautiously about John's interruption of the prologue poem (John 1:1–18) with his insistence that John the Baptist is not the

Christ. Does this mean that there is some question about this central matter at the time of John's writing? Are there followers of John the Baptist who may yet be apart from the gospel of Jesus Christ? This second level of historical quest is helpful for study, but must be engaged in only modestly.

3) *The theological question.* Now we are at the point of the study where we ask the implication questions. First, what does it all mean, especially within its own setting. Second, what great truths are now coming into clearer focus as a result of the text?

4) *The contemporary question* asks of the text its meaning alongside of other world views. When, for instance, I relate the teaching of Jesus to the teaching of Plato, or Philo, or Hegel, I am pursuing the contemporary question.

5) *The discipleship question* asks of the text and of myself what this passage that I am now reading means for my own life, and what is my response to this text?

Let me encourage each of you to write your own commentary upon John's Gospel, perhaps in the form of a journal or daily record of your journey with the book. The following questions are intended to encourage your own reflection. The questions may also act as an aid to group discussion.

* * *

Study 1, John 1:1–18. In the Beginning. What other parts of the Bible do the opening verses of the Gospel remind you of? If you were describing the first eighteen verses in musical terms, what moods, tempos, melodies, come to your mind? If these verses were all you had to go on, what could you learn about the writer's convictions?
In-Depth Question: How would you describe the world view presented in these verses?

Study 2, John 1:19–34. The People's Prophet. On the basis of verses 1–34, what are your impressions of John the Baptist? What role does he take in relationship to Jesus? What insights do you gain into his personality?
In-Depth Question: Draw together the references to John the Baptist in Matthew, Mark, Luke, and along with John's account develop your own explanation of the message of John and also a character study of his personality.

Study 3, John 1:35–51. The Disciples. What are your reactions to this first encounter of Jesus with the first group of his disciples? Are there any surprises for you? What is it that impresses Nathanael about Jesus? Have you had in your own experiences any similar kinds of encounter dynamics as Nathanael?

In-Depth Question: Collect all references to the disciples in John's Gospel, and develop a personality sketch of the individual ones mentioned on the basis of John's record.

Study 4, John 2:1–12. Invitation to a Wedding. What is happening in the relationship between Jesus and his mother? If you used this incident as your evidence, what does it show you about Jesus? Why do you feel the disciples were so impressed?

In-Depth Question: Trace throughout the Gospel John's use of the word *glory*. Develop your own definition of John's intent and meaning for that word.

Study 5, John 2:12–25. The Temple Incident. Does the sentence, "What sign do you have to show . . ." interest you? What do you think the people mean by that question? How do you react to Jesus' answer? Why are the people upset by his response? Do you ever want God to give you a sign? Why or why not?

In-Depth Question: Compare John's account of the temple cleansing with the Synoptic Gospels. Reflect upon the complicated reaction of the people.

Study 6, John 3:1–21. Encounter with a Pharisee. Reflect upon your own impressions of how Nicodemus might feel about his dialogue with Jesus. What did he hear that might alarm or disappoint him? At the same time, what did he hear that might encourage him? What does Jesus teach about the Holy Spirit in this encounter?

In-Depth Question: Look at all the references to the Pharisees throughout this Gospel. Who are they? What is their historical origin, beliefs? What is their relationship to Jesus? Why are they so interested in Jesus?

Study 7, John 3:22–36. Friend of the Bridegroom. What is John the Baptist's response to the question asked him about cleansings? Why does he answer in this way?

In-Depth Question: On the basis of the first three chapters of John, answer this question: Who is Jesus Christ? What about him impresses you most deeply?

Study 8, John 4:1–42. The Samaritans. In this dialogue of Jesus with the woman at the well, trace the stages of the encounter. What are some of the levels of encounter that you sense? What discoveries does the woman make? What about the disciples and their response?

In-Depth Question: Trace in this Gospel the encounters and dialogue of Jesus Christ with women. How does he relate to women? Are you surprised at our Lord's stance? Compare his dialogue with Nicodemus with this incident. What differences do you see?

Study 9, John 4:43–54. A Man from Capernaum. How do you feel about the negative reply to this man? What does the man's response to Jesus tell you about him? Does this incident teach you something for your own life?

In-Depth Question: Trace the use of the word *sign* in John's Gospel. On the basis of the references you find, draw up your own description of what you feel the word means in John's Gospel.

Study 10, John 5:1–15. The Lonely One. What are some differences you detect between the healing accounts in Study 9 and Study 10? How would you describe the psychological-spiritual outlook of the man by the Pool of Bethesda prior to his healing? What would you have advised the man at the pool to do?

In-Depth Question: Survey the miracles of Jesus, as recorded in John's Gospel, and draw up some of your observations about these incidents.

Study 11, John 5:16–47. Four Witnesses. What reasons do you find from this text to explain the opposition of some toward Jesus? How do you understand the claims that Jesus makes in this setting?

In-Depth Question. Trace the Sabbath dispute throughout John's Gospel that develops between Jesus and the leaders of the people. Are there deeper issues at stake? What relevance does this have to your life today?

Study 12, John 6:1–15. The King Everyone Wanted. This miracle is recorded in all four Gospels. Why do you think this sign is so impressive to the writers and the people? Why do you feel that Jesus withdrew when the people wanted to honor him as king?

In-Depth Question: Put together some picture of the Messianic expectations of the people on the basis of evidences you have discovered up to this point in the Gospel of John. What kind of a leader are you looking for?

Study 13, John 6:16–24. A Storm. Try to feel with the disciples of Jesus. How would you describe the mixture of feelings that they have following the feeding of the five thousand and Jesus' response to the crowd? What happens in the shipboard incident as far as the disciples are concerned?
In-Depth Question: Trace throughout John's Gospel the phrase "It is I" *(Greek, ego eimi)*. Draw up some of your own reflections upon the use of this simple expression by Jesus throughout the narratives.

Study 14, John 6:25–71. The Hard Words. Why do you feel that some of Jesus' followers turn away from him at this point? Why are they disappointed? Do you find Jesus' words difficult to understand? Why? Try to put them into your own language and experience.
In-Depth Question: Trace to this point in John's Gospel some of the statements and/or acts of Jesus that seem to you to be hidden, indirect, not obvious. How do you explain these hidden statements/ acts of Jesus? Why do you feel that he teaches in that way?

Study 15, John 7:1–36. Problematic Jews. Why does John say that the brothers of Jesus did not believe in him? In the light of the dialogue recorded here, how would you define what John means by the word *believe*? Why has Jesus created such controversy among the people?
In-Depth Question: Do you sense in the text of John, up to this point, that Jesus Christ has been put under the pressure of temptation? Compare such accounts if you find them in John with temptation of Jesus found in the Synoptic Gospels.

Study 16, John 7:37–52. The Living Water. Why does Jesus ask questions of people? What is your reaction to our Lord's use of the word *water*?
In-Depth Question: With the aid of a dictionary of the Bible, or other resource books on the first-century period, study the practices and ceremonies of the yearly feasts of the Jews.

Study 17, John 7:53–8:11. The Kingly Silence. Why does John call this event a temptation of Jesus? Why the silence of Jesus—

why did he not answer the accusers' question? What do the people learn from Jesus—the onlookers, the accusers, the woman?
In-Depth Question: Up to this point in John's Gospel, how have Jesus' acts related to his words? Trace the event/acts of the Lord and reflect upon what they say in themselves.

Study 18, John 8:12–30. The Light of the World. How do you personally react to the word *light?* What does it mean when Jesus calls himself "the light of the world"? How has Jesus Christ been your light?
In-Depth Question: Compare the references to *light* in John 8 and John 1 with the Psalms (e.g. 27:1), and comment on your findings.

Study 19, John 8:31–59. Way of Freedom. What is Jesus teaching about light? About truth? Who do you feel were some of the people offended by Jesus' promise concerning freedom? What would it mean to you to be free? What are you bound by?
In-Depth Question: Jesus touches a raw nerve for some of his listeners with his reference to Abraham. What is he teaching here? Why is this teaching so explosive?

Study 20, John 9:1–41. A Question of Blindness. Does the question asked by the disciples of Jesus intrigue you? Look at the total narrative. What happens to the man healed? What are some of your feelings toward the whole incident—toward the man, the disciples, the leaders in the temple, Jesus?
In-Depth Question: What role do the disciples of Jesus have in the ministry of Jesus? Trace this question through the first nine chapters of John.

Study 21, John 10:1–42. The Good Shepherd. Reflect upon the brief parable that Jesus teaches. How does Jesus describe himself? What are some things you learned about Jesus and his purpose in this passage? How do they relate to your own life?
In-Depth Question: Compare the use of parables in John's account and in the Synoptic Gospels. Why do you think Jesus used stories, images, figures, in his teaching?

Study 22, John 11:1–44. The Bethany Incident. Note the dialogue of Jesus with Martha. What does she believe? How does Jesus guide her faith? Comment upon Jesus' answer to Martha, "I am the resurrection . . ." What is the significance of this statement for us today?

In-Depth Question: Look through the four Gospels for Jesus' relationship to this family of Lazarus in Bethany.

Study 23, John 11:45–57. Conspiracy. How do you explain the hostile reaction of some of the leaders to this event and toward Jesus? What are your reactions to the statement of Caiaphas?
In-Depth Question: Trace throughout John's Gospel up to this point the objections and arguments that have been made against Jesus.

Study 24, John 12:1–19. The People's King. How do you respond to this incident? to each of the characters in the event? What has Jesus shown of himself in this event? How do you explain the popularity of Jesus on Palm Sunday?
In-Depth Question: Judas Iscariot appears in this incident. Develop your own study of this person on the basis of the four Gospels' narratives.

Study 25, John 12:20–36. A Hard Parable. How do you interpret the brief parable about the grain of wheat? In what ways does Jesus Christ draw people to him?
In-Depth Question: Trace through John's Gospel to this point the way Jesus describes his relationship with God.

Study 26, John 13:1–30. The Servant Lord. What has Jesus shown about himself in the foot-washing incident? What has he taught about the way of discipleship in this event? How does this relate to our life today?
In-Depth Question: Develop a character study of Peter as John has portrayed him in this Gospel.

Study 27, John 13:31–38. The Lonely Valley. How do you explain the sentence "Where I am going you cannot follow..."? What is it that Jesus must do alone? Why? What commandment does Jesus give?
In-Depth Question: Up to this point in John's Gospel, what has Jesus taught about the significance of his death and victory? Has his teaching been hidden or obvious?

Study 28, John 14:1–14. "In My Father's House." Why, at this point in the narrative, might the disciples be troubled? What are the promises that Jesus makes in this text? What has he taught about the way of discipleship? How do his promises and his teaching relate to your life?

In-Depth Question: Relate the "I am" passages in the Gospel of John to events in the ministry of Jesus. Do you find a relationship?

Study 29, John 14:15–31. The Holy Companion. What are some promises that Jesus makes in this text? How will he fulfill these promises? What role are the disciples to have? Do these promises have meaning for you?

In-Depth Question: Trace through John's Gospel the teaching about the Holy Spirit.

Study 30, John 15:1–11. "My Joy in You." What does Jesus teach in the image of the vine about himself? about his disciples? about his will for their lives? What is the fruit? What impresses you about the word *abide*?

In-Depth Question: Trace throughout John's Gospel to this point teachings and events that show you what Jesus means by the word *love*.

Study 31, John 15:12–27. "You Are My Friends." What would you say are the ingredients in Jesus' definition of *friend*?

In-Depth Question: Draw together your discoveries in the Book of John thus far as to the meaning of discipleship.

Study 32, John 16:1–15. The Witness to Justice. How does Jesus describe the ministry of the Holy Spirit (Counselor)? What do you feel is meant by the phrase "convince the world of sin and of righteousness and of justice." How might this teaching change the way you relate to others?

In-Depth Question: Draw together from John's Gospel an explanation of the word *sin*.

Study 33, John 16:16–33. The Disciples and the World. Why will the disciples weep? How do you interpret the parable of Jesus about the woman giving birth? What does Jesus teach is the source of the disciples' joy? How can there be joy in the middle of tribulation?

In-Depth Question: Trace through John's Gospel the teaching of Jesus about prayer. What words does he use? How would you describe the relevance of the teaching here on prayer for your own life?

Study 34, John 17:1–26. Prayer for the Disciples. What themes from earlier parts of the Gospel are drawn together in Jesus'

prayer? What specific requests does Jesus pray for his disciples? Do you see a relationship between themes in this prayer and the *Our Father* Prayer taught by Jesus in Matthew 6?
In-Depth Question: Trace the references in John to evil and the evil one. Are some indirect, hidden? What is the teaching concerning the evil one?

Study 35, John 18:1–11. The Night. What are your reactions to this event? Why does Jesus decline Peter's act?
In-Depth Question: Compare this arrest incident with the account as recorded in the other Gospels. Why do you think that each is somewhat different?

Study 36, John 18:12–40. A Trial. Why do you feel John records the denial of Peter and in such detail? What are the questions put to Jesus by Pilate? Give your own reflections on this dialogue. What do you think Pilate meant by his question "What is truth?"
In-Depth Question: How would you describe the difference between the kind of death Jesus experiences as recorded in the Gospels, and the death of a person at the hands of a rioting mob?

Study 37, John 19:1–16. Ecce Homo. How do you understand Jesus' statement to Pilate in verse 11? How is Pilate persuaded to agree to the crowd's demand? Try to put yourself into the psychological pressures of that morning.
In-Depth Question: Compare the trial narratives in the four Gospels and develop a character sketch of Pontius Pilate.

Study 38, John 19:17–30. The Humiliation of Jesus. Read the other Gospels' account of Jesus Christ's death. What are facts about the event of the cross that John particularly notes? How do you interpret the sentence, "It is finished"?
In-Depth Question: Comment upon the seven last words of Jesus as recorded in the four Gospels. What do they tell you about Jesus and about the ultimate significance of his life and death.

Study 39, John 19:31–42. Jesus Is Dead. What do you feel is the significance in John's narrative of the soldier's act in verses 34–37?
In-Depth Question: What is the meaning of the Cross? Reflect theologically and personally upon this question.

Study 40, John 20:1–23. On the First Day. Each Gospel records that the women were first to discover the reality of the victory of

Jesus Christ. How do you explain that each Gospel's account is different? What features in the encounter of Mary and Jesus most impress you?

In-Depth Question: Why do you feel the victory of Christ is so important a part of the message of the early Christians? How is it important to you?

Study 41, John 20:24–31. Thomas the Twin. What does the Risen Jesus give to his disciples? How do you feel about the promises of Jesus to the disciples? What are Thomas' doubts? What happens that resolves his doubt?

In-Depth Question: What do Thomas's doubts mean to you? Why do you think his skepticism was recorded?

Study 42, John 21:1–25. The Intimate Gospel. How would you describe Peter's state emotionally and spiritually as chapter 21 opens? What happens to change him? How do you interpret the threefold questions of Jesus? What do you think are the goals John had in writing this Gospel?

In-Depth Question: What has the Gospel of John meant to you personally in your own discipleship journey?

Bibliography

Albright, W. F. "Recent Discoveries in Palestine and the Gospel of John." In *The Background of the New Testament and Its Eschatology*. Edited by W. D. Davies and D. Daube. New York: Cambridge University Press, 1964.

————. *New Horizons in Biblical Research*. New York: Oxford University Press, 1966.

Barrett, C. K. *The Gospel According to St. John*. London: SPCK; New York: Seabury Press, 1960.

Barth, Karl. *Dogmatics in Outline*. New York: Harper & Bros. 1958.

————. *Evangelical Theology: An Introduction*. New York: Holt, Rinehart & Winston, 1965.

Bonhoeffer, Dietrich. *The Cost of Discipleship*. 2nd edition. New York: Macmillan, 1967.

————. *Letters and Papers from Prison*. Rev. and enlarged ed. Edited by Eberhard Bethge. New York: Macmillan, 1972.

————. *Life Together*. Translated by John W. Doberstein. New York: Harper & Row, 1976.

Book of Confessions of the United Presbyterian Church U.S.A. 2nd ed. 1970.

Brown, Raymond E., ed. *The Gospel According to John*. 2 vols. Anchor Bible Series. New York: Doubleday, 1966, 1970.

Bruce, F. F. *New Testament History*. New York: Doubleday, Anchor Books, 1972.

Bultmann, Rudolf. *The Gospel of John: A Commentary*. Translated by G. R. Beaseley-Murray. Philadelphia: Westminster Press, 1971.

Burney, C. F. *The Aramaic Origin of the Fourth Gospel*. Oxford: Clarendon Press, 1922.

Calvin, John. *Commentary on the Holy Gospel of Jesus Christ According to John*. 2 vols. Grand Rapids, MI: Wm. B. Eerdmans, 1949.

Chesterton, G. K. *Orthodoxy*. New York: Doubleday, Image Books, 1969.

Dodd, C. H. *The Interpretation of the Fourth Gospel*. New York: Cambridge University Press, 1953.

————. *Historical Tradition in the Fourth Gospel*. New York: Cambridge University Press, 1965.

Dostoevsky, Fyodor. *The Brothers Karamazov.* New York: Random House, 1955.

Guillaumont, A., et al. *The Gospel According to Thomas.* New York: Harper & Bros., 1959.

Hoskyns, E. C., and Davey, F. *The Fourth Gospel.* 2nd ed. Naperville, IL: Alec R. Allenson, 1956.

Jeremais, Joachim. "The Present Position in the Controversy Concerning the Problem of the Historical Jesus." *Expository Times* 69 (1958): 333.

Käsemann, Ernst. *New Testament Questions of Today.* Translated by W. J. Montague. Philadelphia: Fortress Press, 1969.

Lewis, C. S. *The Horse and His Boy.* New York: Macmillan, 1970.

⸺. *The Lion, the Witch and the Wardrobe.* New York: Macmillan, 1970.

⸺. *Miracles: A Preliminary Study.* London: Geoffrey Bles; New York: Macmillan, 1947.

⸺. *The Screwtape Letters.* New York: Macmillan, 1964.

⸺. *The Silver Chair.* New York: Macmillan, 1970.

Lightfoot, R. H. *St. John's Gospel and Commentary.* Edited by C. F. Evans. New York: Oxford University Press, 1956.

Manson, T. W. *Studies in the Gospels and Epistles.* Philadelphia: Westminster Press, 1962.

Micklem, Nathaniel. *Behold the Man: A Study in the Fourth Gospel.* London: Geoffrey Bles, 1969.

Milik, J. T. *Ten Years of Discovery in the Wilderness of Judea.* Naperville, IL: Alec R. Allenson, 1959.

Morris, Leon. *The Gospel of John.* Grand Rapids, MI: Wm. B. Eerdmans, 1970.

Palmer, Earl. *Love Has Its Reasons.* Waco, TX: Word Books, 1977.

⸺. *Salvation by Surprise.* Waco, TX: Word Books, 1975.

Pannenberg, Wolfhart. *Jesus, God and Man.* Philadelphia: Westminster Press, 1968.

Pascal, Blaise. *Pensées.* Translated by W. F. Trotter. New York: Random House, 1941.

Sartre, Jean Paul. *The Words.* New York: Fawcett World Library, 1975.

Schlatter, Adolf. *Der Evangelist Johannes.* Stuttgart: Calwer Verlag, 1930.

Schnackenburg, Rudolf. *The Gospel According to St. John.* 2 vols. Translated by K. Smyth. New York: Herder & Herder, 1968.

Shirer, William L. *The Rise and Fall of the Third Reich.* New York: Fawcett World Library, 1976.

Tolkien, J. R. R. *The Fellowship of the Ring.* Vol. 1 of *The Lord of the Rings.* Boston: Houghton-Mifflin, 1967.

Westcott, B. F. *The Gospel According to St. John.* Grand Rapids: MI: Wm. B. Eerdmans, 1954.